Making Connections

25 Stories for Sharing Faith with Teens

Kass P. Dotterweich

Hi-Time*Pflaum
Dayton, OH 45449

Making Connections
25 Stories for Sharing Faith with Teens
Kass P. Dotterweich

The Scripture quotations contained herein are from the *New Revised Standard Version Bible:* Catholic Edition, © 1993 and 1989 by the Division of Christian Education of the National Council of the Churches of Christ in the U.S.A. Used by permission. All rights reserved.
Design: Linda Becker
Illustrations: Tom Girard
©2000, **Hi-Time✳Pflaum**, Dayton, OH 45449
Permission to photocopy stories for use with participants is granted to the buyer. No other use of this text is granted without the permission of the publisher.
ISBN 0-937997-58-7

Contents

Introduction 7
Faith Sharing 10

Stories

Abuse 14
Anger 17
Being Sexually Active 20
Boundaries 23
Cheating 26
Competition 29
Computer Chat Rooms 32
Depression 35
Divorce 38
Evangelizing 41
Gossip 44
Peer Pressure 47
Pornography 50
Prayer 53
Prejudice 56
Relocation 59
Running Away 62
Shoplifting 65
Skipping School 68
Smoking and Drinking 71
Stealing Money from Parents 74
Suicide 77
Superstitions 80
Talking with Parents About Tough Issues 83
Vandalism 86

DEDICATION

To all whose tireless and faithful commitment

to the faith formation of young people

is an inspiring real-life response to the gospel.

Thank you!

Introduction

Talking with teenagers can be an exciting and challenging experience. The challenge is in getting started. Teens will relax and open up if they are given a safe opportunity for sharing and exploring. They will listen, ask questions, and share their own life experiences. The key, of course, is to minimize risk.

Risk of what? Teens fear judgment. Their world is expanding, their bodies are changing, their values are in a state of flux. They are surrounded with change. What they once trusted now seems undependable and unpredictable. They want to question, explore, discover, but they want to do this within an environment that will not leave them feeling diminished in some way.

Teenagers can understand that there are vague and gray dimensions of life—that's what makes them such challenging and exciting people. They feel an urgency about defining—for themselves and the world around them—who they are, given life's unknowns. In that process, they want to walk into the midst of all that is confusing to find that which they can claim as part of themselves. Watching this process can be frightening and frustrating for the adults who care for these soon-to-be adults. Our own life experiences have given us some "inside" information that we want to give these young people so they don't have to learn "the hard way." Noble as this desire is, however, teenagers must be free to explore—and the safest way for them to explore is in dialogue with their peers and those they trust. When this dialogue happens within the framework of a faith environment, young people are afforded the added opportunity to begin building the foundation of morals and values that will ground their entire lives.

Faith Sharing

Faith Sharing

The truths and tenets of our Christian faith are deeply rooted in storytelling. Generation after generation, beginning with the stories of the people in the Old Testament and continuing throughout the New Testament, stories were told and retold to help people grasp and understand the meaning of life, salvation, and the power of God. Stories let us express what we've experienced and, in that expression, we have the opportunity to understand ourselves and life around us. We grow up with stories, and they remain a vital part of our ongoing growth throughout life. When you listen closely to the dialogue of teens, you will find, again and again, that they're talking about something that happened to them or someone they know. They're telling their stories.

Storytelling is a good way to initiate faith sharing with teens. Listening to a story, teens hear things that are familiar, disturbing, encouraging, insightful. As they explore the details of a story, they are better equipped to organize their own thinking, to make parallels between the story and their own lives, and to find where faith comes to bear on every aspect of life.

Young people will find the following short stories relevant to their lives. Each one describes dilemmas, confusions, and choices teenagers face every day. From a safe distance, young people can examine, criticize, and identify with the details and personalities in these stories. The discussion questions that follow each story serve to take young people deeper into the situation described, giving them the opportunity to explore options and discover dimensions of faith and moral values that they can take into their own lives.

Here are some guidelines for directing discussion with young people.

Set Parameters

Establish a request-to-speak technique that will keep interruptions at a minimum. This may be as simple as requiring those who wish to speak to raise their hands, but it could also be something more creative. For example, consider giving a Bible to each young person. The Bible remains on the floor until the person wants to speak, at which time the person picks up the Bible and holds it up until called upon.

Explain to the group that there are no right or wrong, good or bad comments, questions, or answers in a discussion. Everyone's input is valuable.

Let the group know how long the discussion will last, and respect the

Faith Sharing

limit you set in place. Teens seem to have an inner timing mechanism that informs them when to join in.

Reassure the group that disagreement and debate are not only acceptable, they're good. Everyone is given the opportunity to learn something new when conflicting opinions are respectfully expressed in a discussion.

Keep the Discussion Moving

Listen for those comments that begin with "I think" and "I feel." These are key statements that give you permission to ask questions: Why do you think that? Why do you feel that? What has been your experience? What do you do when you feel...?

Involve those young people who are not participating by asking them questions: When have you had a similar experience? When have you felt like that? If someone doesn't respond with this kind of prompting, however, do not insist.

To help young people explore options, use questions such as: What else? Is that the only way to...?

Don't rush to get through all the questions at the end of each story. Faith sharing is not goal-oriented; it is driven by substance. Stay with any one question until you feel that the point has been exhausted.

• Summarize

Good discussions need closure. Having established for yourself how long the discussion is to last, allow time to summarize what's been shared. This need not be a detailed summary and it need not include comments that everyone made. Generalizations are sufficient.

• Photocopying

For your convenience, you are free to make as many copies of each story and its accompanying discussion questions, *Take Another Look*, as you need for your group. You need not get written permission from the publisher for this purpose.

Stories

Abuse

The Abbotts lived in a small farming community in the southern part of the state. Mr. Abbott worked for the city government and Mrs. Abbott worked for the bank. Their daughter, Charlene, was in eighth grade, and their son, Roger, was a high school senior. Roger had applied and been accepted to State University, and was looking forward to going to college. Mr. and Mrs. Abbott were active in their community, and the kids had lots of friends.

Monday mornings were always hectic at the Abbott household. Monday morning would dawn and no one was prepared to start the week after a long and busy weekend. Everyone needed the bathroom at the same time; everyone scrambled to find lost items; everyone bustled in the kitchen to get a quick breakfast before dashing out the door. Needless to say, this kind of hectic routine often left everyone in a bad mood.

"Come on, Charlene! How much longer are you going to be?" yelled Roger to his sister through the closed bathroom door. "You've been in there long enough. Even if you stayed in there another hour, you'd still be just as ugly! Give it up and get out!"

"Shut up, Roger!" Mr. Abbott snapped. "You should talk about being ugly! Ha!"

"Where are my car keys?" yelled Mrs. Abbott. "I left them right here on the counter. I know I did. Who took them? Someone must have taken them—they wouldn't just walk off by themselves. I know one of you kids took them."

"You'd lose your nose if it weren't attached," said Mr. Abbott with a chuckle, amused at his own humor.

Just then, the bathroom door banged wide open and Charlene stomped out. "Nose? Well, I'm going to bust someone's nose the next time they use all my shampoo!"

"I have a meeting tonight after work," Mr. Abbott announced. "I'll be home late."

"Oh, great!" sighed Mrs. Abbott. "You wanna tell me how this is going to work? You have a meeting and I have to work late. How's Charlene supposed to get home from piano lessons?"

"Walk," snapped Mr. Abbottt, "or run or crawl. I don't care. You should have thought of that before now. I don't know why she has to go on with those stupid lessons anyway. She's got no talent and the lessons are only wasting good hard-earned money."

"Shut up, Dad," snapped Charlene. "I am so good and I am not wasting money. At least I don't go throw a bowling ball down the lane to knock over ten stupid looking things—and pay for the *fun* of it, like some people!"

With one swift continous motion, Mr. Abbott stepped toward Charlene and slapped her across the mouth. "You don't talk that way to me, young lady. Do you hear me? I'm your father and I demand respect!"

"Well," smiled Mrs. Abbott with satisfaction, "she's got a point. You have to admit."

Just as quickly, Mr. Abbott turned to Mrs. Abbott and put his face right into hers. "She doesn't have a point and you don't have a brain."

Mr. Abbott's anger was obviously on the rise—and this scared Roger. Grabbing his father's shirt sleeve, giving him a shove, and spinning him away from his mother, Roger said, "Go on, Dad. Get out of here. Go to work."

"Mom," screamed Charlene, "make 'em stop! You can make 'em stop. Don't just stand there like an idiot! Make 'em stop!"

"Shut up, Charlene," snapped Mrs. Abbott

Abuse

with her fists clenched. "This doesn't have anything to do with you or me. This is between your father and your brother. Now just mind your own business."

Pulling away from his son, Mr. Abbott yelled, "Oh, I'm going all right. I'm going. And that meeting tonight might just last a few days!"

"Fine!" responded Mrs. Abbott, "Just leave enough grocery money and your meetings can last a month! I don't care!"

"Grocery money?" Mr. Abbott sneered. "Grocery money? I don't think so. You all eat too much anyway. All three of you are as fat as sows! What you got here to eat is plenty. You'll just have to manage. I'm out of here." The door slammed closed behind him.

The kitchen seemed deeply quiet for five brief seconds.

Then Mrs. Abbott snapped at Charlene and Roger, "Go on, you two. Get going. You just stand around like you've got all day. Lazy! You're just plain lazy. You think if you mope long enough I won't make you go to school 'cause it's too late. Well, that just shows your feeble-mindedness. You're going to school."

"Oh yeah, Mom," replied Roger. "I guess we're just supposed to go on as usual and pretend that good old Dad just kissed us all good-bye and headed off to work with a smile and a wave. Come on, Mom. What are you? Old and stupid and blind and deaf? That man is going to hurt one of us bad one of these times and you just want to keep on ignoring it."

"And you don't add to it, I guess. Is that what you're saying, young man?" asked Mrs. Abbott. "You think grabbing your father and shoving him around isn't part of the problem? Both of you kids just drive us nuts. We've got our jobs, this house, and you kids to take care of, and you've got the nerve to think your father is the only one with a problem?"

"Here we go again," whined Charlene. "I've heard this sob story so many times it makes me sick. Who's the problem? Who's not?"

"Part of the problem? Me? Oh yeah. It's me and Dad, isn't it?" yelled Roger. "We're the problems. You two are just a couple of goody two shoes, aren't ya? Well, I got news for you. The old man has a problem and we're all his victims. He gets away with his abuse and we all just have to take it like mice afraid of the big bad cat. Well, not me. No, sir! I'm not taking it anymore. The next time he lays a finger on me or opens that big mouth of his to me, I'm going to let him have it."

"Shut up, Roger. You're no better than he is," screamed Charlene.

"And neither of you know what you're talking about," said Mrs. Abbott. "Now for the last time, finish getting ready and get out of here. I'm sick of the two of you trying to place blame and make a big deal about this every time it happens. You'd think this was some kind of wild animals' den that wasn't safe for human beings. We've got our home and our health. You start whining about things and that's sinning! If you can't be grateful to the good Lord for all the good you got and just take the bad along with the good, then you're selfish sinners! Now, where are my keys?"

• • • • •

Mr. Abbott came in late that night, long after the rest of the family was in bed. In the morning, he apologized to the family for his behavior. He explained some of the stress he was under at work and all the responsibilities he'd taken on for the city's Chamber of Commerce. He explained that all he needed was a little more peace and quiet around the house and a little appreciation for all he did for the family.

Abuse

Take Another Look

What is the difference between a person who engages in abusive behavior and a person who is merely in a bad mood?

Besides physical abuse, what other kinds of abuse can you name?

Where do you see these other kinds of abuse demonstrated in the story? Give specific examples.

What would you do if you knew that a friend of yours was being abused in some way?

Mrs. Abbott says, "If you can't be grateful to the good Lord for all the good you got and just take the bad along with the good, then you're selfish sinners!" Do you agree or disagree with this statement? Why?

"This is my commandment, that you love one another as I have loved you."
John 15:12

Anger

Ramon and Adam were seniors in high school and worked at Sellie's Cafeteria. Although the work was hard, Ramon and Adam liked working at the cafeteria because their boss was fair and respectful and the pay was good. In the five months they had been employed there, both had received raises for being quick and responsible.

When Ramon first was hired at the cafeteria, his father helped him finance a car. Ramon had to make regular payments to his father for the car, and he had to handle all repair and maintenance expenses. Ramon was proud of his car and took good care of it. He washed it regularly, cleaning and polishing the inside as well as the outside. Ramon figured that if he kept the car in good condition, he could take it to college with him in the fall. By owning his own car, Ramon had learned a lot about finances, budgeting, and automobile care.

"This is bogus," growled Ramon, kicking a rock out of his way as he and Adam walked to work Saturday morning.

Yeah," sympathized Adam, "but look—didn't you say your dad was going to try to help you find another car?"

"Yeah, Adam, but that's not the point," barked Ramon. "I'm walking because of that loser who hit me. Besides, that car was cool. I really put a lot into it—and now it's just—Bam! Gone!"

"Well, the other guy got a ticket," offered Adam, "so it's not like he got away with anything. Plus, his car was totaled, his insurance will go up, *and* his insurance company has to pay you—but probably not as much as the car was really worth, huh?"

"No, I couldn't put a price on that car," said Ramon with a sigh. "My first car! And I took such good care of it. The whole thing's really messed me up. I've been without wheels now for two weeks—and the thing of it is, the loser who hit me probably just took his sorry self out and bought a brand new Volvo or something—and the jerk didn't even say he was sorry. I mean, he even tried to blame me. He told the cop I was too young to be driving in the first place. I feel like kicking him in the teeth...I really do."

"Well," Adam pointed out, "you can't go kick him in the teeth, Ramon. That's not going to fix anything."

"Well, I could slash the tires on his brand new car...maybe then he'd feel what it's like," snapped Ramon. "Or I could start hassling him. You know, maybe calling him up at 3 o'clock in the morning to be sure he's just as disturbed as I am."

"Man, what's the matter with you, Ramon?" asked Adam. "None of that stuff is cool. You looking for revenge or something?"

"Sure, I'm looking for revenge!" shouted Ramon. "Why not!"

"Why not?" said Adam in as calm a voice as possible. "Because revenge isn't going to change a thing for you. You're not going to feel better if you make this jerk feel rotten."

"Oh yeah?" said Ramon. "Well, I gotcha there, bud, because I know I *would* feel better if he felt lousy! I want him to be as hassled as I am."

"But why?" pushed Adam. "I don't see what good that's gonna do."

"I'm really mad, Adam," shouted Ramon, "and I need to do something about that."

"W-e-l-l," offered Adam cautiously, "there are things you can do that aren't destructive."

"Oh, Mr. Calm and Cool, here," said Ramon

Anger

with a bitter sneer. "I guess you're going to tell me to run it off...or work it off at the gym? Is that it?"

"Sure, Ramon," Adam agreed. "You could do that. Or you could just keep talking to me about how mad you are...that helps...'cause I can hear ya, man...it's bogus. You're right about that."

"Well, you're being a good bud, Adam, but I'm

> **You're saying that if I could just talk to this jerk...I might feel better about things?**

talking and I just seem to be getting madder and madder, the more I talk to you," Ramon said.

"Well, besides revenge, what would help?" asked Adam.

"I don't know," said Ramon, trying to respect Adam's question. "I just wish I could let that guy know how mad I am...I guess that's really it. In the mess of everything that day, I didn't get a chance to tell that loser how I felt about his stupid driving and his idiot way of ignoring how I felt. And I haven't talked to him since then...it's just his insurance company that calls."

"Hey, that's a good idea, Ramon," suggested Adam. "Why not do that? Just give the guy a call and tell him how you feel. You can do that without trying to make him feel like a jerk...even though he might be one."

"So, let me get this straight, Dr. Cool," said Ramon, beginning to lighten up a little. "You're saying that if I could just talk to this jerk, tell him how I felt on the day of the accident, and let him know how important that car was to me, I might feel better about things?"

"I think it's worth a try, Ramon," encouraged Adam. "I remember when my dad was spitting mad at our neighbor for mowing down some stupid flowers along our driveway. I didn't really see what the big deal was, but my dad was frosted, I tell ya. He went right over to the neighbor's front door and told him that he had worked hard to get those flowers to grow there, that the flowers were special to him, that he'd have to start all over, and that he was mad about the whole thing."

"Man," said Ramon, "did the other guy bust your dad's nose?"

"No," continued Adam, "the guy didn't know my dad felt that strongly about those flowers. He said he just didn't give it a thought...he just mowed 'em down. Today, we're still good friends with our neighbors, even though Dad really blew his cool that day."

"Hmm," pondered Ramon, "I wonder if my dad would go with me to talk to this guy?"

"Well, will ya listen to yourself?" observed Adam. "That's the first time you've referred to the person who hit you as a guy instead of as a jerk or a loser. I think you're on to something."

· · · · ·

That weekend, Ramon and his father went to see the man who had hit Ramon's car. At first, the man didn't seem to want to talk to Ramon and his father, but Ramon asked if he could just have five minutes of his time. Reluctantly, the man said, "Okay." Ramon then told him how much he liked his car, how he worked hard to make payments on it and to keep it clean and in good condition. He explained that it had been his first car and that he was really proud of it. Before Ramon began to say how really mad he was, the man interrupted him and said, "Gee, kid, I'm sorry. Your first car, huh? Man, I remember my first car...what a beauty! I was really proud of her too. You know, I'm really sorry."

Anger

Take Another Look

Name at least three things that contributed to Ramon's anger about the loss of his car.

Identify at least two good pieces of advice that Adam offered Ramon.

What are some destructive ways people deal with their anger?

What are some constructive ways people deal with anger?

Why does talking about emotions often help?

As shoes for your feet put on whatever will make you ready to proclaim the gospel of peace.
Ephesians 6:15

Being Sexually Active

Sherry and Leon were seniors in high school. They started dating when they were sixteen and started going together at the beginning of their senior year. They cared deeply for each other and often talked about what it would be like to spend the rest of their lives together. Sherry had been accepted at State University and wanted to study physical therapy. Leon was going to Community College to study accounting.

Sherry and Leon enjoyed kissing and touching, as they made discoveries about their own and each other's body. They also knew the importance of respecting one another and the beauty of sex. At times, however, one of them would "push the limit," as they called it, and suggest intercourse. Those were difficult moments because their emotional and physical feelings would be deeply aroused.

"I don't want you to do anything you don't want to do, Sher, so don't get me wrong," said Leon. It was Friday night, and Sherry and Leon were driving home from the movies. He was "pushing the limit."

"No, no. It's okay, Leon," Sherry said gently. "I won't do anything I don't want to do. I just don't want us to do something we're going to regret."

"Now you're sounding like all the abstinence talk," Leon said. "I never did really get that part anyway...what's to regret? If we have safe sex, and we love each other, what are we going to regret?"

"See, that's just it. There's a lot more to safe sex than just making sure no one gets pregnant. We *don't know* what we're going to regret. I don't completely get it, either. But I think there's something to all that stuff. I mean, well...here's how I sometimes think about it. If it were a sweltering hot day and I wanted to take a nice cool dip in a mountain lake—and someone I trusted told me not to do that because I'd *regret* it—because the water moccasins would eat me alive—I'd go ahead and suffer the heat."

"But we're not going to get eaten alive by making love, Sher. You know that," said Leon.

"But we may get hurt in some way, Leon... that's what I'm saying," repeated Sherry "People we trust tell us that, and I believe it...even though my emotions and my body really want something else. Sex is just something really, really big that we don't know a lot about. We know how to 'do' it and all that, but we don't really know how we're going to feel afterward."

"So now you're going to bring in the old commitment stuff, I guess," said Leon, trying to be understanding.

"Yeah, something like that," said Sherry. "In a commitment, two people get...well... naked...all the way...not just physically. They share everything in life."

"We share everything, Sher, don't we?" asked Leon.

"No!" said Sherry very quickly and emphatically.

"We don't?" asked Leon perplexed.

"No, we don't, Leon," insisted Sherry. "Look...we don't share a home. We don't share finances. We don't share work. We don't share families. We don't share big worries...we don't even *have* big worries. All that's part of commitment, I guess, and I think having sex fits into sharing all that stuff. That's being naked all the way."

"What if we made that commitment right here—right now?" asked Leon.

Being Sexually Active

Sherry shook her head. "That doesn't work, Leon, and you know it. Remember when we promised to help each other study hard in chemistry last semester? Did we keep that simple promise? No-o-o. And you know why? Because we didn't tell anyone else. We didn't turn to others to *help us* keep that promise. When people make commitments, they turn to others to help them keep that commitment. My mom and dad say that if they hadn't had their families and friends to help them through the first years of

There's a lot more to safe sex than just making sure no one gets pregnant.

being married, they never would have made it."

"I really like your mom and dad, Sher. Did I ever tell you that?" asked Leon. "They...well, they just seem to have such a good time together...it's like they're really great friends instead of being married to each other."

Sherry laughed. "That's it! They *are* best friends, and that's why they're such a great couple! They're together for life. Anyone who knows them knows that. They love each other and they love life. I want to be just like that some day, Leon—and it might be with you. But I'm not so stupid as to think that, at seventeen, I know I can be like that for the rest of my life with you. I like to daydream about that. I like to fantasize about that. But I *don't know* that right now. And what I see my mom and dad having is not worth losing because I grab at something right now that I'm not really ready for."

"Do you think your mom and dad were virgins on their wedding night, Sher?" asked Leon.

"I don't know, silly," laughed Sherry, "and it's not really any of our business, now is it? But...do you want to be a virgin on your wedding night, Leon?"

"Well...that's a good question, and I guess I never really gave it much thought," admitted Leon sheepishly. "I can see how cool that would be...I mean, my wife and I discovering things together—for the first time. I mean, when I think about doing that with you, man—awesome!"

"I think about that, too, Leon," said Sherry, as she put her arm around the back of Leon's shoulder. "I would feel so proud to discover you and let you discover me...making discoveries no one else has ever made. I mean, when I think about how exciting that would be, I can't even tell you how I feel."

"It'd be...like...," Leon thought for a minute. "I guess it'd be like some kind of special gift we give each other that we've never given anyone else. It would be like the Super Bowl of celebrations on our wedding day, I guess."

. . . . .

The next morning, Sherry wanted to sleep in, but her mother woke her. "Come see what's on the kitchen table for you." Sherry crawled out of bed, grabbed her robe, and made her way to the kitchen to find a bouquet of a dozen yellow roses. The card said, "Waiting for the Super Bowl. Love, your best friend, Leon."

Being Sexually Active

Take Another Look

What does Sherry mean when she says that there's a lot more to safe sex than just making sure no one gets pregnant?

What do you think about abstinence? Why?

Why are some people afraid to say "no" when they are pressed to have sex?

Why does the Church teach that intercourse belongs exclusively within marriage?

How does a faith community support a married couple's commitment?

Let love be genuine; hate what is evil, hold fast to what is good; love one another with mutual affection; outdo one another in showing honor.
Romans 12:9-10

Boundaries

Karen was a junior in high school. She had lots of good friends, but she felt especially lucky to have the best friend in the world—her mother. She could talk with her mother about anything. If she was worried, scared, or just wanted to know something, she could go to her mother and they could talk. Even though she and her mother didn't agree on things like clothes, makeup, and music, they could talk about what they each liked and didn't like. Karen especially appreciated the way her mother asked questions and then listened carefully to the answers. This made her feel that her mother wanted to understand Karen and help her make good decisions in life.

"Mom," asked Karen, "can you run me over to Holly's house?"

"Sure, hon," said Karen's mother. "Do you want me to drop you off there—or what?"

"No, no," explained Karen. "I just need to run in for a minute. Holly didn't go to school today because she wasn't ready for the history test, so I went to each of her teachers and got her homework assignments for her. I have to drop off her assignments and some of her books. And then I have to go by the library to take back her overdue books because she spilled Coke on one of 'em, and she's afraid she's going to get in trouble."

"Hey, sweetie! Hold on a minute," said Karen's mother with a gentle smile. "What's going on here? It sounds like you're doing a lot for Holly that Holly should and could do for herself."

"Well, she's just in a few binds, Mom, and I'm trying to help her out," explained Karen.

"Hmm," Karen's mother commented. "I think something else is going on here."

"What are you talking about, Mom?" said Karen. "What's going on?"

"Well, first of all, I think there's a difference between being in a 'bind' and being in a 'mess.' I define a 'bind' as a set of circumstances that come together, kinda by coincidence. If I'm in a bind, I've done my best, but things beyond my control have put me in a bind. But a 'mess,' well, that's where I'm not taking on my own responsibilities and I've ended up with a mess. It sounds to me as if Holly is in a few messes rather than binds, and frankly, dear, you're not helping her out much."

"What do ya mean, I'm not 'helping her out much,' Mom?" asked Karen. "I think I'm being a pretty good friend. If she doesn't get her homework turned in, she'll get zeroes for that day's work...and as for the library book...well, if the librarian yells at me, I can just tell her that I'm returning the book for a friend, and that I don't know anything about the Coke spill."

Karen's mother sighed. "Karen, can't you see that you've taken on someone else's problems and responsibilities? Holly didn't 'miss' school, she 'skipped' school. And even if spilling the Coke on the library book was an accident—and I'm sure it was—it's Holly's responsibility to offer an apology to the librarian and to face whatever fines she might have to pay."

"But if I don't help Holly, Mom," said Karen with a slight whine, "I'll feel like I'm not being a very good friend."

"Honey, friends *help* friends face life's struggles—they don't face life's struggles *for* them. There are things called 'boundaries,' Karen, and I would describe boundaries as those invisible lines around us that separate the things that are mine to take care of from the things that belong to others for them to take care of. We are not good friends

Boundaries

to others—and we don't take good care of ourselves—when we get our boundaries confused."

"So, Holly doesn't have good boundaries, huh, Mom?" asked Karen.

"Well, that's what I see," observed Karen's mother. "Holly is pushing off onto you the things that belong to her—but there's more to it. You seem to be willing to *let* Holly get out of taking care of her own responsibilities...which means you need to look at how strong *your* boundaries are."

"You mean that what feels like a helping hand," asked Karen, "may not be a helping hand at all?"

"Exactly," explained Karen's mother, "and

Friends help friends face life's struggles—they don't face life's struggles for them.

that can be risky sometimes. You want to lend a helping hand, but you want your friends to be the best they can be by taking care of their own responsibilities. When you try to set good boundaries for yourself, some people get angry or they let their feelings get hurt. I've even seen friendships break up because of boundary issues."

"Well, what should I do about Holly, Mom?" asked Karen.

"What do you think you should do?"

"Hmm," Karen was thinking out loud. "I think I'll take Holly's homework and books to her, but I'm going to tell her that because it's important for her to go to school, I won't help her skip school anymore. Then I think I'll tell her that she'll have to return the library books herself because even if spilling the Coke on the book was an accident, she has to take on the responsibilities that go along with the privilege of using the library."

"That sounds like good boundary-setting to me, dear," Karen's mother agreed. "Are you ready to go?"

• • • • •

A few minutes later, Karen's mother was waiting in her car on the street in front of Holly's house.

"So what did Holly say?" Karen's mother asked when Karen got back in the car.

"Oh, she was cool with it," said Karen with a confused look, "but her mom went ballistic. Holly said she could see my point on both the homework stuff and the library books, and she even gave me a hug and said 'thanks.' But her mom heard us talking, and she just really went off on me. She yelled, 'What kind of a friend are you anyway?' She said that Holly just asked me to do a few little favors and that I just couldn't be bothered."

"What did you say, Karen?" asked her mother.

"I just said, 'Whatever. See ya tomorrow, Holly,' and I got out of there."

"Well," observed Karen's mother, "I guess we can see how Holly might have to struggle to learn about boundaries, huh?"

Boundaries

Take Another Look

Define "good boundaries" in your own words.

How can people learn to set good boundaries for themselves?

How can poor boundaries ruin a friendship?

How can you tell if you're being selfish or if you're setting good boundaries?

How does having good boundaries make us loving and strong Christians?

All must test their own work; then that work, rather than their neighbor's work, will become a cause for pride. For all must carry their own loads.
Galatians 6:4-5

Cheating

Justin was a junior in high school. He made average grades and put average effort into his school work. He figured if he could just get Cs on his report cards, his parents and teachers would stay off his back and he'd get by. High school just didn't mean a great deal to Justin. He was going to join the army when he graduated, and he just wanted to get through high school, graduate, and get on with the rest of life.

Justin was having a hard time with chemistry, though. Since the beginning of the semester, he'd gotten Cs and Ds on every quiz, and he hadn't turned in his experiment report. He knew that the grade on his final semester exam would count for seventy-five percent of his grade for the semester. He could still pull a C for the semester, he figured, if he could pass the semester exam. The problem for Justin was that he'd lost his textbook, and studying for the test was nearly impossible without the text. Fortunately, his chemistry teacher, Mrs. Parks, had agreed to lend him her text for the weekend. He had to return it Monday afternoon, before the exam.

On Saturday afternoon, Justin sat on the floor in his bedroom, leaning up against his bed. With his headset securely in place, his favorite music playing, and the chemistry textbook in his lap, he was ready to study. He knew the exam would cover chapters eleven through eighteen. All he needed to do was read the material, make a few notes, memorize a few terms and formulas, and he'd be set...enough, at least, to make a C, which is all he needed.

As he opened the textbook to chapter eleven, a handful of folded papers fell from the back of the book.

"Hmm," Justin wondered out loud, "what's this?" At first glance, the papers looked like handwritten notes and questions. But the last three pages were neatly typed and organized, and at the top were the words: *Final Semester Exam.*

"Oh man," thought Justin. "Parks put a copy of the exam in her book. This is great! This is just too good! It's all right here! Who needs to study the text when you've got the exam right in front of you! This is going to be a breeze."

Justin began to read the test carefully. He knew the answers to some of the questions, but he had to check the text for a lot of them. On a separate sheet of paper, he made notes about the things he'd have to memorize.

"Hi," said Justin's sister, Emily, as she came into his room to borrow his CD player. "What's up?" she yelled so Justin could hear her over his music.

Taking off his headset and quickly shoving Mrs. Parks' exam under the bed, Justin answered, "Studying for my chemistry exam."

"And you study for your chemistry exam by shoving papers under your bed? Come on...what are you really doing?" Emily asked again.

"Come on, Em, knock it off," Justin said a little nervously. "I'm studying...see...here's the textbook."

"That's the textbook, okay, and under the bed is...?" Emily asked again.

"Take your face out of mine, Em, or I'll take it out for you, you hear me," threatened Justin.

"Oooh, looks like old Justin's up to some-

Cheating

thing," said Emily. "Come on, what's under the bed? If you don't tell me—well, I'll just have a chat with Sarah about your little rendezvous with Dretta last week."

"That's blackmail, Em!" yelled Justin. "You're stooping to blackmail. What's it to you, anyway? I'm studying here and you're not helping with your big nose in my business."

"Fine," said Emily with a threatening grin, as she headed out the door with Justin's CD player. "Whatever."

"Wait," said Justin at the last minute. "Okay, just don't tell Sarah anything about Dretta, okay? Just keep your big mouth shut...about that, and this too," Justin said as he pulled the chemistry exam from under his bed. "Old Lady Parks let me borrow her textbook so I could study this weekend, and look," he said, holding the exam out for Emily to see. "She left a copy of the final exam in the book."

"Oh man, Justin," said Emily, "and you're cheating!"

"I'm not cheating," insisted Justin. "I'm just going over the exam that Parks was stupid enough to leave in the book."

"You're cheating, Justin," insisted Emily. "You're the stupid one...you're cheating."

"How can you call this cheating?" demanded Justin. "It's not like I went looking for this. I was studying...and...literally...the exam just falls into my lap. I'm an absolute and total idiot if I don't take advantage of a good opportunity, Em. You'd do the same thing, and you know it!"

"Well, I don't know about that, Justin," said Emily. "Nothing like that's ever happened to me. But it *is* cheating. You get to study the exam ahead of time, which is something none of the other kids get to do."

"Oh, I see," said Justin with a laugh. "So, if I pass the exam around to the other kids so I don't have some advantage they don't have, then I'm *not* cheating? Is that it?"

"N-o-o," said Emily slowly, trying to think things through for herself as she went along. "It's not that...it's just that...it's not fair. The whole idea of an exam is to see what you've learned. You and Parks aren't going to know anything about what you've learned if you cheat."

"Well, call it what ya want, Em," Justin said. "I'm just taking advantage of an opportunity like anyone else would. It's not like I'm going to have a cheat-sheet up my sleeve or anything. I'm studying just like everyone else. It's just that I know exactly what to study. There's no cheating involved."

• • • • •

Justin awoke with a start on Monday morning, the day of his chemistry exam. His first thought was, "Oh man...the exam! The textbook! Do I return the textbook *with the exam in it* or do I *ditch* the exam? If Parks realizes the exam is in the back of the book, she's going to know I studied it. If I don't leave the exam in the book, and she asks me about it...oh, I could tell her that I never saw anything like it...that there wasn't anything in the book when she gave it to me. Yeah, yeah...that's what I'll do. I'll trash the exam. I never saw it." Justin got out of bed and looked at himself in the mirror. With the most intense and serious expression he could come up with, he said to his reflection, "Why, no, Mrs. Parks. I don't know what you're talking about."

Cheating

Take Another Look

How is cheating a form of stealing?

Why do people cheat?

Why does Justin insist that he isn't cheating?

What tells you that Justin knew he was, in fact, cheating?

What would you have said to Justin if you were Emily?

Happy are those who observe justice,
  who do righteousness at all times.
                    Psalm 106:3

Competition

Mr. Knoll had been coaching varsity basketball for seventeen years. He had fifteen winning seasons and five state championships to his credit. He was proud of his record and the high school administration was proud of his accomplishments as well. Although Mr. Knoll drove his team hard and demanded excellence, players respected him and learned a lot from him as a coach. In seventeen years, six boys from his team had gone on to college on basketball scholarships. Getting on the team was a great opportunity.

"So you want to play basketball," said Mr. Knoll to the group of young men waiting to try out for the team. "Why? Anyone? Why? You, what's your name?" he asked, pointing to a young man sitting on the front row of the bleachers.

"Oh, I'm Will Reynolds," the boy stammered.

"Reynolds, why do you want to play basketball?" Mr. Knoll repeated.

"Well, I like it and I think I'm good at it," responded Will with confidence.

"And what makes you think you're good enough for this team, Reynolds?" Mr. Knoll asked in return.

"I work out a lot and I've watched the team play. I know I can play as well as anyone on the team right now, Coach," responded Will, still with confidence.

"Well, Reynolds—and this goes for the rest of you too—working out and knowing you can play as well as anyone else on the team isn't good enough," shouted Mr. Knoll. "You gotta play *better* than anyone else on the team! Ya gotta be a winner—and ya gotta *know* you're a winner. You, there, what's a winner?"

Travis Seasons shot back, "A winner is someone who practices hard, really plays his best, and is dedicated to teamwork."

"Wrong," shouted Mr. Knoll. "Somebody tell me what a winner is!"

Cody Toris shot his hand up. When Mr. Knoll nodded at him, he responded, "A winner is someone who knows he can win and keeps that in mind at all times."

"Wrong again," shouted Mr. Knoll. "A winner is a winner! Do you hear that? A winner wins—and the scoreboard will tell you every time if you're a winner or not. All ya gotta do is keep your eye on that scoreboard and it'll let you know every second of every game whether or not you're a winner! It tells you and it tells the rest of the world 'there's a winner' or 'there's a loser.' The scoreboard tells the whole story from start to finish and every second in between. It knows more than you do at any

I want to win, but it's just not the most important thing to me. There's just so much more.

point in the game. It knows who you are, how you play, and whether you're a winner or a loser. It's an honest judge, too, do you hear me? It doesn't lie! It says, 'You scored, you winner,' or 'You missed, you loser.' So, Reynolds, are you a winner?"

"Well," stammered Will, giving in to his sense of humor, "I'm not sure about that right now, I guess. The...um...the...scoreboard isn't on."

A rumble of laughter came from the young men gathered on the bleachers, but Mr. Knoll wasn't amused. "Smart alecks are not winners, Reynolds!" he said sternly. "The scoreboard

Competition

isn't interested in your wit, your mind, or anything else about you. It doesn't give a rat's nose about your charm, your looks, your life. Its sole purpose is to let you know if you're a winner or a loser."

"Daniels," Mr. Knoll snapped at a boy who'd been on the team for two years, "are you a winner?"

"I'm a winner, Coach!" responded Adam Daniels. "I accumulated 273 points last season. I'm a winner!"

"You got it, Daniels. You're a winner," said Mr. Knoll. "You, Kritts," he said, pointing to another boy who'd been on the team for three years, "Are you a winner?"

"I'm a winner, Coach!" Mark Kritts shot back. "I've accumulated 573 points in 54 games!"

"There ya go," said Mr. Knoll. "Now there we've got some winners. Let's see if we've got any more. Come on...let's see what ya guys are made of."

• • • • •

That evening, Will and Travis talked about the basketball tryouts.

"So what do ya think, Will?" Travis asked. "Did ya make the cut?"

"I don't know," Will said. "But I was 'on,' I know that much. I mean, like, I was hot. It's like I couldn't miss, so if the scoreboard had been on, it sure would have told Coach that I'm a winner, and that's what he's looking for. So, yeah, I think I got a real good shot at it. What about you?"

"Yeah, well," said Travis, "I did good—but that whole scoreboard thing. That really got me. I mean, I got so wigged out over all that...I don't know...I guess I just don't get it, ya know? What's that all about? It just seems like something's missing there. Knoll didn't seem to want to hear anything about skill or practice or teamwork or doing our best."

"Aw, come on, Trav," said Will. "You heard the man and he's right on. The only thing that counts at the end of the game is the final score, ya know what I mean? Ya win or ya lose, and the idea is to win. If ya start thinking about all that other stuff, ya lose focus. Ya gotta make the shot, get the point, go the distance, win!"

"But where's the fun in it, Will?" asked Travis. "I mean, I love basketball. I just love the feel of the ball in my hands, the moves on the floor, the push to be my best...and yeah, that's got something to do with winning...but keeping my eye on the scoreboard? Letting it drive me? Letting it tell me whether I'm a winner or a loser? I mean, what about teamwork? We gotta work together. It seems to me like the *team* has to be in there somewhere...working together and all that. I don't get it."

"Well, good buddy," Will laughed, "if you want to make the team, you better figure it out... and I don't think Knoll could be any clearer. Winning is everything."

"I just don't see it that way," said Travis, "...so maybe I'm just not cut out for the team. I mean, I want to win, but, like, it's just not *the most important thing* to me. There's just so much more."

"Well, you might be right," said Will, "Maybe you aren't cut out for the team 'cause Knoll is looking for winners, and you're just not a winner—at least it doesn't sound like it to me."

Competition

Take Another Look

How does competition bring out the best in people?

How does competition bring out the worst in people?

What does Travis mean when he says, "There's just so much more"?

Besides games and sports, where do we find competition in our culture?

What would be a healthy Christian attitude toward competition?

Pursue love and strive for the spiritual gifts....
1 Corinthians 14:1

Computer Chat Rooms

Marty was a senior in high school. For the first three years of high school, Marty had lots of friends, was involved in sports, and had a good part-time job. Then, for his seventeenth birthday, Marty's parents got him a computer. They thought that Marty would use the computer mainly for school work, but they also knew that he'd enjoy computer games and surfing the Net. Marty invested himself in his new computer. He got hooked on the games...and he got hooked on the Net.

"Come on, Marty," whined Tasha, Marty's younger sister. "You promised I could play BlipBall with you this afternoon."

"I know, I know," said Marty, without looking away from the monitor, his fingers flying over the keys. "But not now...later. Go away."

Twenty minutes later, Marty's mother stuck her head into his room. "Marty," she said, "don't forget to bring your trash downstairs. Your dad is leaving for the recycling center in about ten minutes."

"Okay. Okay, Mom," Marty responded, without looking away from the monitor, his fingers flying over the keys.

Five minutes later, Marty's brother yelled, "Mart! Phone!"

"Later!" Marty yelled back, without looking away from the monitor, his fingers flying over the keys.

Five minutes later, his father strolled into his room. "Marty, didn't your mother tell you I'm leaving for the recycling center and that you should bring your trash downstairs?"

"Yeah, Dad. Yeah, later...er...I mean...just a sec," said Marty, without looking away from the monitor, his fingers flying over the keys.

"Marty?"

"Yeah, just a sec, Dad."

"Marty?"

"Yeah, wait a sec. Here, just let me finish...I'm just about finished...I'm wrapping it up."

"Marty?"

Finally, Marty could hear the frustration and impatience in his father's voice. He turned to look at his father, his eyes leaving the monitor and his flying fingers finally stopping for the first time in half an hour.

"What, Dad? What do you want?"

"Did you hear your little sister?" his father asked.

"No, what does she want?"

"Did you hear your mother?" his father asked.

"No...I don't know...yeah, maybe...oh yeah, the recycling. Here. I got it right here. I'll just get it together," Marty said as he made a move to get up.

"No, just stay right there, Marty," his father said, holding up his hand to motion Marty back into his seat. "I want to talk to you."

"Right now, Dad? I mean...I have to get this stuff all together for you to take to...."

"Not right now, Marty," his father interrupted. "Will you just listen to me for a minute?"

"Oh yeah...sure...what's up?" asked Marty.

"Marty, are you listening to me? Are you paying attention?" Marty's father asked.

"Well, yeah...sure...I mean, I know you'll make it quick, whatever it is...I have to get back to the chat room, you know. I don't want to miss anything, but I know you're in a hurry, too, so if you'll just let me get to the trash, I'll...."

"Marty!" his father raised his voice. "Calm down! I'm *not* in a hurry and I'm *not* here to talk to you about the recycling. I want to talk to you about your computer. Something isn't right here and your mother and I are worried."

"Worried? About the computer? It's working fine. I love it. Don't worry," Marty said, feeling his impatience rising.

32

Computer Chat Rooms

"No, Marty," his father said with exasperation. "We're not worried about the computer. We're worried about you *and* the computer. It's obvious that you're enjoying it, but you're...well...it's almost like you're hooked on it...like it's an addiction."

"Oh, that," said Marty, realizing what his father was trying to say. "Well, yeah...I guess I'm on the computer a lot...but that's why you gave it to me. Right? I mean, I'm doing papers on it and I'm finding out all kinds of things on the Web. It's really great. The chat rooms, of course, are the best. It's just so much fun, Dad, to go in there

> **Real relating, real friendship, real life— all take the whole person, not just words sent back and forth by modem.**

and meet all these really wonderful people and find out what they think and what they do. I never had so many great friends. They're just the greatest. It's almost like I didn't know what really good friends were like until I met these people in the chat rooms."

"But look at what's going on around you, Marty," said his father. "You lost your job because you showed up late one too many times—because you kept taking 'one more minute, one more minute' in the chat rooms. You quit the team because you didn't want to put in the long hours of practice when you could be here in front of the computer. You're not doing things with your friends anymore. You're losing it, kid, and your mom and I are going to have to do something if you can't get a grip on this."

"But Dad," protested Marty, "it's not like I needed that job, or that sports were all that important to me. And so what if I don't do things with my friends anymore. Look at it this way...I'm home more now. That ought to make you and Mom happier. No more late hours, no more worrying and wondering where I am. Hey, we haven't had a fight about curfew or my having the car in...what...months!"

"But Marty," said his father slowly, "don't you see how you leave real life behind when you go into those chat rooms?"

"Oh, no, Dad," insisted Marty. "See, you just don't get it. It's like I *go into* real life when I go into the chat rooms. I just feel so alive, so me, so real! It's like everything else just becomes a bother."

"It feels that way because the chat rooms are more fantasy than real, son," his father explained. "Sure, there's a human being sitting at a keyboard somewhere responding to you, but it isn't real relating, don't you see? Real relating, real friendships, real life—all take the whole person, not just words sent back and forth by way of modem. The real you is right here in front of me."

. . . . .

A week later, Marty's coach called him into his office. "Marty," he said. "I want you to do something. I want you to consider coming back to the team."

"Me? Why, Coach?" asked Marty, somewhat surprised.

"Because you're a real team player, Marty. You're a good athlete," explained the coach. "Most of all, though, you're good for the rest of the team. They look up to you, Marty. They respect you. You have a way of bringing out everyone's best...and that's a real asset to a team. Will you just think about it, Marty?"

"Sure," said Marty, feeling a rush of life that he hadn't felt in months.

Computer Chat Rooms

Take Another Look

What are the benefits of computer chat rooms?

What are the drawbacks of computer chat rooms?

How are computer-chat-room friendships incomplete—what's missing?

Why did the coach's request to Marty to think about coming back to the team make him feel "a rush of life"?

How might computer chat rooms be a good way/place to share your faith with others?

...and you show that you are a letter of Christ, prepared by us, written not with ink but with the Spirit of the living God, not on tablets of stone but on tablets of human hearts.
2 Corinthians 3:3

Depression

Melissa and Cathy were sophomores in high school. Although they had known each other through their freshman year, they didn't have an opportunity to spend much time together. Now, as lab partners in sophomore biology, they were becoming good friends. They enjoyed the same kind of music, and they both liked in-line skating.

"I just about had ya there, Mel," huffed Cathy, catching up with Melissa at the top of hill in the park. "I just couldn't get the speed I needed, though, to get up this hill."

"Yeah, I got a real break," smiled Mel. "I saw this hunk at the top of the hill, and I just said to myself, 'Go get him, Mel, old girl.' And I took off!"

"Hmm," teased Cathy, "wouldn't that be considered illegal...using your drug of choice for an advantage?" Both girls laughed as they tumbled onto the grass for a rest.

"I have to get going in a minute," said Melissa. "I promised my mom I'd go to the doctor with her today."

"Oh," said Cathy, "I didn't know your mom was sick."

"Yeah, she's got depression," said Melissa. "The doctor changed her medication, so she has to go in for a checkup every week now to see if the new prescription is the right one."

"What do you mean 'she's *got* depression'?" asked Cathy. "You make it sound like it's a disease or something."

"That's exactly right, Cath," explained Melissa. "Depression is a disease. When someone gets depression, it has to be treated just like an illness."

"Treated? You mean with medicine and all that?" asked Cathy, somewhat bewildered.

"Oh yeah...medicine and other kinds of therapy. It's really awful, Cath," said Melissa. "I feel so sorry for my mom sometimes. You know, it's like life is just too much for her. Before she started getting help, she'd stay in bed...sometimes for two and three days at a time. She wouldn't have any energy for anything...even eating. She'd lose weight, she couldn't concentrate, she'd burst out crying for no reason...it was just awful. I mean, Mom wouldn't even go to church, and that was always something really important to her."

"Oh man," exclaimed Cathy. "That does sound awful."

"Yeah, and you know what made it even worse," Melissa said, with a sad shake of her head, "is that my dad and I just didn't understand. We'd yell at her and tell her to snap out of it. We didn't know she was sick or anything...we just kinda thought she was being moody or something...you know, like she was having a bad hair day, or something. We just kept going on about how she needed to get a job or start a hobby or exercise more...we just didn't know...and she didn't either. None of us knew. Mom just cried or slept all the time and my dad and I just got madder and madder. After a while, we could tell that it sure was more than having a bad hair day."

"Well, how did you find out that your mom was sick?" asked Cathy.

"I'm actually the one who figured it out," said Melissa with some pride. "I was sitting in the dentist's office...you know, waiting the usual two hours for my appointment. I picked up this magazine about health and saw on the cover that it had an article in it about skin care. But while I was trying to find the article, I came across this stuff about depression. In big words at the top of the page it said something that I'd heard my mom saying a lot, 'I don't know what's the matter with me!' I mean, Cath, it was like my mom

Depression

was yelling at me from the pages of the magazine."

"So the article said depression is a disease?" asked Cathy with respectful concern and interest.

"Exactly! It kept using the words 'illness' and 'disease,' and it talked about all kinds of things that were just like what my mom was going through."

We didn't know she was sick or anything...we just kinda thought she was being moody or something.

"So you told your mom about the article?" asked Cathy.

"Well, eventually," said Melissa, "but first I went to the library...and man, there are a lot of books about depression. Some of them were like medical books...real big and fat...but I found one that wasn't very long, thinking that if my mom would read even little bit of it, she might decide to go to the doctor. So, I checked it out, took it home, and asked my dad to take a look at it. He's actually the one, then, that got Mom to read it."

"So your mom went to see the doctor after reading the book?" asked Cathy.

"Well, not at first," Melissa admitted. " She was so glad to find out that other people felt the same way she did...so I guess that alone made her feel better...but not for long...so that's when she finally went to the doctor."

Cathy thought a minute, then started to ask, "Do you suppose depression is something older people get because...."

But Melissa interrupted Cathy before she could finish her question. "Hold on, Cath! Depression is something *anybody* can get *at any age*. You and I could get depression, your younger brother could get depression. It doesn't have anything to do with age. And you can't say someone gets depression 'because.' There's a lot of research being done on depression, but there's nothing definite that's been pinpointed as the cause."

"Wow, Mel," said Cathy with admiration. "You seem to know a lot about this stuff."

"I *do* know a lot about it, Cath," said Melissa, "and I want to keep finding out more. I mean, depression is really a dangerous disease. I want to know everything I can find out about it so I can help my mom...and so that I'll know what's happening to me or anyone I know who might get depressed."

· · · · ·

With time, Melissa's mother improved. She worked with her doctors to find the right medication, the right dosage, and the right kind of therapeutic treatment. When Melissa became a senior, she got a part-time job working for the daily newspaper and volunteered to write a feature on depression and teenagers. The feature was so popular that the newspaper reprinted it in a small pamphlet and made it available at no cost to local mental-wellness clinics and the high school guidance counselor's office.

Depression

Take Another Look

What does Cathy learn about depression from Melissa?

How can people be disrespectful of those who suffer with depression?

Why is it important for Melissa and her dad to learn everything they can about depression?

From what Melissa told Cathy about her mother, what would you identify as some of the symptoms of depression?

How can you help someone you suspect suffers with depression?

O Lord, God of my salvation,
  when, at night, I cry out in your presence,
let my prayer come before you;
  incline your ear to my cry.
                    Psalm 88:1-2

Divorce

Scot was a freshman in high school and a good student. Although he enjoyed sports, his main interest was scouting. He would become an Eagle Scout in six months. Scot liked and respected Mr. Byran, his scoutmaster. When Scot had a hard time earning certain badges, Mr. Byran would offer him extra help.

In recent weeks, Mr. Byran had noticed that Scot wasn't showing his usual enthusiasm. In fact, Scot had missed a number of meetings, which wasn't like Scot at all.

"Scot, you need a ride home after the meeting?" Mr. Byran asked Scot one rainy night.

"Well, I'm supposed to call my aunt and have my dad come get me," said Scot.

"You call your aunt to have your dad come get you?" asked Mr. Byran.

"Well...er," stammered Scot. "Yeah, it's stupid. But yeah. That's right."

"What's stupid, Scot? Is something wrong?" Mr. Byran asked gently.

Scot turned away as his eyes started to tear. He really didn't want to talk to anyone, but he goofed. He'd said something he shouldn't have. He decided to just say the rest of it out loud— for the first time. "My mom and dad are getting a divorce. My dad moved out last week and is living with my aunt." With that, he could feel tears on his face.

"Oh, Scot. I'm sorry to hear that," said Mr. Byran, putting his arm around Scot's shoulders. "I can see that you're really upset with this. How are you doing?"

"I hate it! I hate them! It's all just stupid," Scot said, raising his voice. "They just fight about stupid things and say stupid things. They don't have time for us kids anymore— everything's just crazy. They're just being mean and selfish. They don't care about anything anymore."

"Divorce is a painful thing for everyone, Scot," Mr Byron agreed. "But your mom and dad are probably hurt and scared. They don't know what's going to happen so they just seem to be doing stupid and selfish things right now."

"Well, why can't they just quit?"

"Sometimes that's just not possible, Scot. Sometimes we just cannot do what we might want to do with all our hearts. Your parents got married and intended to spend the rest of their lives loving each other. But they just can't do it."

"But why not?" asked Scot, trying to dry his tears. "I just want to know why they can't go on loving each other. They're both good people."

"Of course, they're both good people," agreed Mr. Byron. "They're both great people. But 'why not?' is a question only your mom and dad can answer, Scot. Even they might not be able to answer it right now. It might take years for them to figure out 'why not?' Right now, they just have to focus on how to get through one day at a time. They're angry and scared, just as you are, and they've got big decisions to make. More than anything, they need your love and you need their love right now. I know your mom and dad, Scot, and you've got their love—no doubt about that! I know it's hard, but just keep this in mind—*you* are not being divorced. Your mom and dad will make the best decisions they can right now, and they have the good of you and your brothers right there in the middle of their hearts. They just have so many things they have to figure out right now."

"What am I going to tell my friends, Mr. Byran?" Scot asked, almost in a whisper. "None of them know that my parents are getting

Divorce

divorced? I don't know how to face 'em."

"Look, Scot," said Mr. Byron slowly and carefully. "Who among your friends have parents who are divorced?"

"Well, Jake's parents are divorced. So are DJ's. And our neighbors got divorced last year," responded Scot.

"Do you like any of those people any less because of the divorce?" asked Mr. Byran. "Do you think there's something wrong with those kids because their parents are divorced? Do you think their parents are bad people now that they're divorced?"

"Well, no, not exactly," said Scot. He was afraid he was going to cry again. "But I don't know very much about any of those people. I know my mom and dad, and I know they don't have to get a divorce. I just know it."

"You might believe that, Scot," said Mr. Byran, "but your believing it doesn't make it a fact."

"It's so quiet without Dad around, though," said Scot. "I just know that Mom misses him."

"Well, if your mom and dad have been fighting a lot," pointed out Mr. Byran, "it's going to seem quiet, isn't it, when the fighting isn't happening anymore? Your mom might seem quiet, but she might just be taking care of herself. It's been hard for her and your dad, you know. And they've got some hard times ahead of them. This is a good time for you to really be a loving support to both your mom and dad. It would help them both to hear you say that you love them and that you know how hard this must be for them."

"I wish I could just figure out why," Scot continued. "Maybe my brothers and I could fix things if we just knew that."

"Scot, do you think you caused the divorce?" asked Mr. Byran.

Scot hesitated before he answered, "I don't know. I just don't know."

"Well, kids don't cause divorce, Scot," said Mr. Byron. "When a marriage doesn't last, it has to do with the relationship between the two people—not their kids, not their jobs, not their bills. There are only two people who can 'fix' a marriage—the husband and wife."

Scot sank down in a nearby chair and lowered his head to stare at the floor. "Is getting a divorce a sin, Mr. Byran?" asked Scot quietly.

"Are you worried about that?" asked Mr. Byran in return.

"Well, yeah, kinda—yeah, sure," said Scot. "I mean, we learn that marriage is for life and all that. I don't want my mom and dad to go to hell because they got a divorce."

Mr. Byran bent down, took Scot by the shoulders, and looked him in the eye. "Scot, you're going to have to talk to Father Gary about that—and I suggest you do that soon. I know this much, though. Hell is for those people who just do not want to love God—and your parents love God very much."

• • • • •

Scot became an Eagle Scout six months later. The local paper carried a story about him and included a picture of Scot with his mom and dad. Although Scot and his brothers were living with their mom, and their dad lived in an apartment across town, Scot could see the love and pride his parents had for him as he looked at the picture in the newspaper.

Divorce

Take Another Look

Why is divorce so painful?

Besides the couple and their children, who else is affected by a divorce?

What emotions are involved in a divorce?

Why do some kids blame themselves for their parents' divorce?

How do you express love to your parents when they go through a hard time?

Above all, clothe yourselves with love, which binds everything together in perfect harmony.
Colossians 3:14

Evangelizing

All the juniors looked forward to their end-of-the-year retreat because, over the years, it had gained a reputation for being "the best." One thing that made it fun were the surprises. Each year the young people were asked not to talk about what had happened during their retreat so that the experience would be meaningful and powerful for the next year's class of juniors.

The retreat began on Friday night at seven o'clock and ended at four o'clock on Sunday afternoon. It was held at a lodge in the mountains, where people could hike and have quiet time to themselves. After some games and evening prayer on Friday night, everyone had to go to bed early because Saturday and Sunday were busy days.

It was two o'clock. The Saturday afternoon sharing session was about to begin. Mr. Caley asked the young people at his table to quiet themselves for prayer and began, "Almighty God, we're here in your presence today as your creations. You love us and fill us with life. In the name of your son, Jesus, we ask you to bless what we are about to share, that it might draw us nearer to you. Amen."

The five young people at the table responded, "Amen."

"Okay. Now, Dennis, will you read Matthew 28:18-20 for us?" Mr. Caley said, handing an open Bible to Dennis.

Dennis read, "And Jesus came and said to them, 'All authority in heaven and on earth has been given to me. Go therefore and make disciples of all nations, baptizing them in the name of the Father and of the Son and of the Holy Spirit, and teaching them to obey everything that I have commanded you. And remember, I am with you always, to the end of the age.'"

"Thanks, Dennis," said Mr. Caley. "Jenna, can you summarize what that Scripture reading tells us?"

"Um, well...I don't think it's for people like you and me, Mr. Caley," said Jenna. "It's more for the priests. They're the ones who are supposed to baptize—not you and me, so I think it just tells priests what to do."

"Hmm," said Mr. Caley. "So you're saying that you don't think this particular teaching of Jesus applies to us? What do you think about that, Laura?"

"Well, I think it *is* for us," offered Laura. "I mean, first of all, I think everything in Scripture applies to everyone in some way. But I don't think we're supposed to do exactly what the passage says. I think it means we're supposed to convince people to get baptized."

"And how might you do that, Laura?" Mr. Caley asked.

"How might I do that? Like, right now? Me? Well, uh...I guess I'd just tell people that being a Christian is neat and kinda fun and that they should get baptized."

"Can you be specific, Laura, about *how* being a Christian is neat and fun?" Mr. Caley asked Laura.

"Oh, sure, but...well...oh, I don't know. Ya know, I guess that *would* be kinda hard."

"Ken, how would you go about convincing people to get baptized?" asked Mr. Caley.

"I wouldn't," Ken stated flatly. "I don't think it's anybody's business. It's a faith thing and people are free to make up their own minds. If they want to get baptized, fine. If not, fine too. A Jesus freak who runs around asking you if you've been saved and shoving Jesus in your face all the time is nothing but a pain."

"Have you had an experience like that, Ken?" Mr. Caley asked.

"Yeah. My stepsister is like that," explained Ken.

Evangelizing

"She's always running around talking about sinning and being saved...and it cuts nothing with me...it's just a pain. If that's what Jesus is like, then I'm not interested."

"What *do* you think Jesus is like, Ken?" asked Mr. Caley. "And what do you think he's telling us to do in this passage?"

"Oh, I don't know. I guess I think Jesus is kinda like my grandpa," said Ken. "Gramps is cool, ya know. He's just neat. You just feel really good when you're around him. You can tell he really loves you and wants to know how you're doing. He'd do anything for anyone that needed something. I mean, he really likes to help people out. So I kinda think that's what Jesus is like, and that when he tells us to baptize people, he wants us to be like my grandpa...just doing good things...not running around screaming things about sin and being saved and all that."

"Now that's an interesting take, Ken," said Mr. Caley. "Thanks for telling us about your grandfather. He sounds like a great person. Wilma, what do you think Jesus is telling us to do in this Scripture passage?"

"Well, I guess I kinda agree with Ken," Wilma offered. "I mean, I don't think we have to talk about God and carry a Bible around all the time and chase people down to make them be Christian. If we're just good people, other people will see that and maybe want to be like that. Then they might start asking us questions about what we believe and we could just answer their questions. Then, like Ken says, they're free to do what they want. We could tell them a little bit about what baptism means and what it's all about, and they could decide for themselves."

"So are you saying that we shouldn't ever bring up things about faith and belief in God until someone asks us about it?" asked Mr. Caley.

"Well, I guess so," answered Wilma, "but there *might* be times, I guess, when we'd bring it up. I guess, like, maybe at a funeral or something like that. You might say something about God then."

"What about you, Mr. Caley," Dennis asked. "What do you think?"

"Well, I think this is a challenging Scripture passage," said Mr. Caley. "and we've seen right here in our discussion just how challenging it can be...just trying to hear what Jesus is saying. I agree with you, Ken and Wilma, about living lives that are obviously good, loving others, and being willing to talk about our faith and beliefs when others ask. But I think Jesus wants us to take the initiative from time to time...like now, right here. I volunteered to be an adult partner on this retreat because I knew it would give me a chance to hear about other people's experiences of faith—*and* I knew I'd be able to share my own faith too...and my faith is very important to me. My faith gives me a lot of joy and peace, and I want that for everyone. So, I think Jesus is saying to his disciples, who are people of faith, to go share their joy and peace with others—and to be specific about that when they have the opportunity."

· · · · ·

Two weeks after the retreat, Dennis, Ken, Jenna, Laura, and Wilma got notes from Mr. Caley. He thanked each of them for making a big difference in his life by sharing their faith with him.

I pray every morning that I will end the day knowing a little bit more about what it means to love Jesus and to do God's will. Spending time with you on the retreat helped me know Jesus better. My faith is growing; your faith is growing—and together we grow stronger as Christians. If you would ever like to talk more about this, I'd like to hear from you.

Thank you again.

Fondly,
Pete Caley

Evangelizing

Take Another Look

What is evangelization?

Why is evangelization important to faith?

How would you summarize Jesus' teaching in the Scripture passage discussed in this story?

How many different forms of evangelization can you identify in the story?

How comfortable are you with talking about your beliefs and faith?

We know that all things work together for good for those who love God, who are called according to [God's] purpose.
Romans 8:28

Gossip

Neil didn't like his eighth-grade English teacher. He thought Mr. Andrews was "too tough and unfair." Neil complained to his friends that Mr. Andrews intentionally embarrassed him in class and didn't give him a "fair chance" on tests. Some of Neil's friends agreed with him—Mr. Andrews was a tough teacher. Some of Neil's friends, however, really liked Mr. Andrews—which Neil used as "proof" that Mr. Andrews was unfair and played favorites.

On his most recent report card, Neil got a C- in English, with a comment on his behavior, "Needs to show more effort." Neil's parents gave him a long lecture on the importance of understanding and using good English. They even said they would consider the possibility of summer school for Neil if his English grade didn't improve. When Neil tried to tell his parents that he thought Mr. Andrews didn't like him, they wouldn't listen. "Nonsense," they told him. "You just aren't doing your best. You're not trying."

Neil rushed in the back door, ignored his father at the kitchen table, and made a dash up the stairs to his room.

"Neil!" his father called to him. "Come back here. I've got something to show you. There's a story in the newspaper...."

But Neil was already in his room with the door closed, dialing the phone.

"Stu! It's Neil. You'll never guess what I just saw. Check it out, man. You're just never going to believe this, but I saw it with my own eyes. I was on my bike on Bridge Street—been playing *Sega* with Dave—and I was on my way home. Okay, and there he is—Mr. Horseface-Himself-Andrews. And who's with him? Mrs. Phillips. And what's Phillips doing? She's all over him! Man, you wouldn't believe it. She just couldn't get enough of him—I mean, she's hanging on him right there on the sidewalk and all. And he sure didn't mind. He was really into anything she had to offer. I about lost it, man. It was really something."

"Aw, come on, Neil. You've got to be kidding. Andrews? Phillips? Not a chance. He's a dork and she's such an airhead. Besides, they're both teachers and they're both married. I mean, they're always trying to be so straight. They're so uptight. This is too much. Are you sure, man? I mean, it might have been some other people."

"Oh, no," Neil said with a sharp laugh. "It was Andrews and Phillips all right, and there was no doubt what they were doing. They had their heads close together, talking, like they were sharing all kinds of little things no one knows about. I can just imagine what they were saying, probably planning something like, 'your place or mine?'" Neil let out a loud and ugly cackle.

"Man, Neil. This is too much. This is going to be all over school. What a trip! I wonder if *Mrs.* Andrews and *Mr.* Phillips know that you saw them! I mean, they could get fired for something like this, couldn't they?"

"Sure they could, and wouldn't that just be too, too bad! Boo, hoo. So sad. It'd serve 'em right—especially Andrews. He's such a loser, man. He thinks he knows it all. I can't stand

Gossip

him. I'd love to see him lose his job. Listen, I gotta call Dave. He's going to love this."

"Yeah, well, I'm going to call Kelly and Matt. This is too much. Later, man."

Neil called Dave and repeated the story, everything he saw and what he hoped it would all lead to—the dismissal of Mr. Andrews.

Neil felt great. He found it exciting and satisfying to pass on the news about Mr. Andrews and to think about how it would spread through

> **So what if he exaggerated a little about what he saw... he didn't exaggerate much.**

the school and all around town—and what it would mean for Mr. Andrews. He almost felt proud of himself. Somehow, this was justice. So what if he exaggerated a little about what he saw...he didn't exaggerate much. Mrs. Phillips had her arm around Mr. Andrews, and Mr. Andrews offered her his handkerchief. It was obvious they were sharing something pretty special. People coming out of the surrounding stores and the funeral home on the corner could have seen that much—and he was sure they did. After all, Mr. Andrews and Mrs. Phillips didn't try to hide what they were doing. So, maybe she wasn't "hanging on him," but so what?

Neil laid back on his bed and let his imagination take off. He could hear Mr. Andrews being called to the principal's office over the PA system: "Mr. Andrews, please report to the office immediately. Bring your briefcase and all your personal belongings." Neil smiled to himself. How sweet the image was.

Neil was so lost in his fantasy that the knock on his bedroom door startled him.

"Neil, didn't you hear me? Come here. I want to show you something," Neil's father said.

Neil jumped up off his bed and opened the door to find his father standing in the hall holding the *Daily Journal*. "What's up, Dad?"

"You remember Mr. Temple, don't you?"

"Sure, Dad. He was the principal when I was in first grade."

"Remember how he walked you home your first day of school because you were so scared?"

"Oh yeah. I remember. He was pretty cool."

"Well, he died—of a heart attack. They've got this big feature on him in the paper today. The funeral was this afternoon. What a loss. He was really loved by everyone...all the teachers, all the kids...all the parents. He was so devoted to education and to young people. I imagine all the teachers were at the funeral this afternoon. It has to be really tough—losing a person like that who is so admired."

· · · · ·

The image suddenly came back to Neil—Mr. Andrews, Mrs. Phillips, on the sidewalk, walking close, the funeral home nearby, Mrs. Phillip's arm around Mr. Andrews' shoulder, him offering her his handkerchief.

Gossip

Take Another Look

What is gossip?

What kind of harm can gossip cause?

Why does Neil exaggerate the facts about Mr. Andrews and Mrs. Phillips?

Why does Stu believe Neil?

What should Neil do now?

*The lips of the wise spread knowledge;
not so the minds of fools.*
Proverbs 15:7

Peer Pressure

It was October, and Ashley and her mother had just moved to Central City. Ashley's mother was a nurse, and she had found a good job at Central City General. Ashley was enrolled in Central City High School as a sophomore and was working hard to catch up on the work the other students had been doing since the beginning of the school year. She was a good student, so the extra work she had to do wasn't difficult, but it didn't leave her much time to socialize and make new friends. She felt very much alone.

"Hey, Ashley, are you coming to Autumn Fest this weekend?" asked Candy, the girl who sat next to Ashley in English Comp class.

Ashley tried to cover her feelings of surprise and excitement. Someone was asking her to do something this weekend! "Well, I thought I might go. I don't really know what it's all about."

"Oh, it's cool. You'll have a g-o-o-d time, I can promise you that," encouraged Candy.

"Well, what's it all about anyway?" Ashley asked.

"Oh, all the churches and goody-goody groups around town set up their cute little booths to sell food and trinkets," explained Candy, "and you can play games to try to win stupid stuffed animals and junk like that. The really good time, though, is the street dance on Saturday night. They block off Main Street and bring in a real DJ, and we just really chill."

"Cool," said Ashley, who was excited at the prospect of going to a dance and meeting new friends.

"The real action, though," Candy giggled, as she lowered her voice, "is in the alley at the corner of Main and Pine. I mean, after a few songs, the dance gets pretty boring, so a bunch of us just kinda, like, go off to have our own good time."

"Neat," said Ashley. "What do you do?"

"Well, I suggest you just show up and find out," teased Candy, "because it's kinda hard to explain. You just never know what's going to happen. Like two years ago, my friend Dan showed up with a case of beer. It was s-o-o cool. His older brother had gotten it for him, and let me tell you—he was willing to share. It was so great. Then last year, someone had a little bit of pot. Only a couple of us knew about that—but those of us who knew really had a good time."

Ashley began to feel uncomfortable with some of the details Candy was offering. She wanted to go to the dance and she wanted to be cool with the kids, but she wasn't sure about drinking beer and smoking pot. She'd never done anything like that and wasn't sure she

She needed to decide. Join the cool kids? Or stay with the street dance?

wanted to. At the same time, she was lonely, and it felt so good to be talking like friends with someone. "What else happens at the dance?" she asked Candy.

"Oh, at the dance? I guess I don't really know. My parents just started letting me go two years ago, and both years the party in the alley was so much more fun than the dance. I mean, I guess...well...I guess you just dance at the dance. I think you'd have more fun with us in the alley, though. I *know* what happens there, and it's great. But, you know, we usually don't stick around town for the whole dance. I guess I ought to warn you about that. After a while, someone will probably suggest we go out to

Peer Pressure

Sunset Glade...that's the cemetery...and that's what we've done the last two years. We just hang out there, listen to music, pair off and get cool with guys, you know...just kinda hang loose. Oh, last year...it was so funny...I gotta tell ya this. This one guy, Kenny...he found a tombstone that had this crazy name on it...something like Putshed. Anyway, he had some spray paint, and he changed the name to Butthead. It was a blast! Butthead! Get it?"

"Yeah," said Ashley rather quietly, "I get it. Butthead."

"So, ya coming?" asked Candy. "I mean, being new in school and all must be a bummer. I just know you'd have a great time. You'll meet the really cool kids—maybe even get with a guy you really like. Who knows."

"Oh, well, uh, sure...that is if I can come to the dance in the first place," stammered Ashley, beginning to look for excuses not to go. "You know, my mom and I are still unpacking boxes and kinda trying to move in and all that stuff. It takes a long time, you know. But...I...really want to come to the dance, so I'll look for you there."

"Okay," said Candy with anticipation. "But listen. Don't pass this around. You know, the alley party is really for invited guests only. You have to be careful about who gets in on that kind of thing. You invite the wrong people and—well, things can get bad. Oh man, and if our parents found out—or the cops—well, no more Autumn Fest alley parties, that's for sure. So just kinda think it over and really try to come. Okay? I guess I'll just look for you when I get there?"

"Yeah, I guess so," answered Ashley, not at all sure of herself.

· · · · ·

At home that night, Ashley thought about what Candy had said. She really wanted to go to the dance and she really wanted to make friends. She liked Candy, but she wasn't sure that drinking beer, smoking pot, making out with guys, and hanging around in cemeteries was the way she wanted to make friends. She tried to figure out how she could go to the dance but avoid the alley without looking like—what was the word Candy used?—a "goody-goody." Then again, maybe checking out the action in the alley might be a good idea. After all, good friends can show up any time, anywhere, and she didn't have to do the beer and pot. She didn't have to go to the cemetery.

Ashley knew that her mother would let her go to the dance. In fact, her mother would be excited. She'd been encouraging Ashley to get out and meet some kids, and the Autumn Fest was a perfect opportunity. She just didn't want to go without a plan of action. She needed to decide. Join the cool kids? Or stay with the street dance? And if she wasn't going to join the kids in the alley, she needed a good excuse—
she wouldn't want to ruin her chances of making friends with the cool kids.

Peer Pressure

Take Another Look

What is peer pressure?

How can peer pressure be good? How can peer pressure be bad?

When have you used good peer pressure? Bad peer pressure?

What examples of good or bad peer pressure do we find in Scripture?

What would you do if you were in Ashley's situation?

Thus says the LORD:
Maintain justice, and do what is right,
for soon my salvation will come,
and my deliverance be revealed.
                    Isaiah 56:1

Pornography

Graduation was seven weeks away. James was looking forward to the excitement of the day, the summer fun he had planned, and his first year at State University in the fall. His brother, Glen, was a sophomore at State and had promised to introduce James to some of his friends. James was pleased that he and his brother were finally good friends. When they were younger, they used to fight—sometimes getting into actual fistfights. Now that they were older, they enjoyed the same sports and pastimes, and had a good time hanging out together. James was especially glad that he had the opportunity to spend weekends with his brother on campus.

"Okay, J," said Glen to his brother, "I'm off. I'll run over to the library to pick up the books I've got on reserve—then I'll swing back here, pick you up—and we're off to Diaz Hall. You're gonna like those guys, J. They really know how to throw a party."

"Later, man," James said to his brother, who was already halfway down the hall. James was looking forward to the party at Diaz Hall, mainly because that would be his dorm next year. His brother had told him that Diaz was the neatest dorm on campus for freshmen, and James believed him. Each suite was large, housed four students, and had its own bathroom, complete with shower. The common room had a large-screen TV, pinball machines, and a miniature basketball hoop. The top floor of the dorm was a study hall for round-the-clock quiet study.

James decided to make himself comfortable while he waited for his brother. As he sat down on the floor of his brother's dorm room and leaned back against the bed, the rug shifted to expose the corner of a thin magazine. James pulled out the magazine and found himself looking at the cover of a magazine. The woman posing on the cover was naked, but held feathers across certain parts of her body.

James knew about this kind of magazine. His classmates often passed around what they called "nudie magazines," usually commenting on the women's breasts and faces. He always felt a little uncomfortable joining in, but not so much that he wouldn't go along with his friends, just to be one of the guys. But finding this magazine in his brother's room made James more than a little uncomfortable. He flipped through a few of the pages, found himself almost grossed out, and started to put the magazine back under the rug where he'd found it. Just then, Glen came trotting back into the room.

"Forgot my ID.... Hey, so you found my treasure chest, huh, bro?" Glen said with a grin. "What do ya think? Class act, right?"

"Well," stammered James, "uh...yeah...yeah, cool."

"Here," said Glen, taking the magazine from James. "Did ya see the center spread in this one? Look at that...I mean, would ya just feast your eyes on that!"

Again, James stammered, "Uh...yeah... pretty cool."

"Hey, little brother," said Glen in a teasing voice. "Do we have a problem here? I don't see your eyes rolling to the back of your head. I don't hear you breathing deep. What's the deal?"

"Oh... it's...uh, well," James struggled to explain himself. "I guess it just kinda took me by surprise. I mean, I've seen the girly stuff, but this is...well...this is *more*."

"You bet it's more, my man," laughed Glen, "and there's *more* where that came from. A couple of guys here on campus actually publish this

Pornography

thing. They take requests from their subscribers...you know, if you want to see a certain pose or a certain angle or a certain close up....that kind of thing. Then, get this, man. They set up the shot and take the pictures themselves. It's just...well, like, the next best thing to being there, if ya know what I mean. Naturally, a subscription costs a bundle—but as you can see, it's worth it!"

"You mean these guys can find girls around here who are willing to pose for these pictures?" asked James, letting down his guard a little.

"Oh, sure, J," said Glen offhandedly. "But those chicks get paid—I mean, g-o-o-d money. Look, here, see her?" said Glen, pointing to the woman on the cover. "That's Krin. I happen to know her, and she told me that for ten poses, she earned enough money to pay for half her tuition this year."

"You know her?" asked James, more curious than surprised. "She doesn't mind doing this kind of thing?"

"Mind?" said Glen. "Why should she mind? Look at the money she's earning."

"Well," pressured James, "have you ever asked her if she minds?"

"What's the matter with you, J?" asked Glen with a ring of disdain in his voice. "Why would I ask her that? It's obvious, isn't it? She can't possibly mind getting that kind of money. I mean, it's paying her tuition. Asking her if she minds would be really ignorant. It'd be like asking, 'Do you have to take your clothes off for this kind of thing?' It's just obvious—the *naked* truth—she *likes* it," Glen concluded, laughing at his own pun.

"Well," continued James, getting bolder by the minute. "I just don't get it. It's one thing to look at naked women sometimes...but this stuff is so...crude. I mean, tell me, Glen, what do you get out of this? How can this be entertaining or even interesting? It's not real. This stuff doesn't happen in real-life sexual relationships—at least not in ones worth having."

Glen gave his brother a long, silent look, as if he was trying to find a response for James' questions. "Come on," he finally said, dropping the subject abruptly. "Let's go. Come to the library with me, and we'll go to the party from there. Hey—and I just thought of something. Krin'll be at the party. Ask her your stupid questions yourself, if you want."

. . . . .

James didn't see Krin arrive at the party, but he saw her leaving. He was still disturbed by the magazine he'd found and the conversation he'd had with his brother several hours earlier. That's why he didn't feel at all inhibited about running out the door to catch up with Krin. She stopped and turned to him when he yelled her name.

"Hi, Krin. My name's James. I'm Glen's brother. I didn't see you get here."

"Oh, hi, James...J, isn't it? Isn't that what your brother calls you?" asked Krin.

"Yeah," said James. "He's the only one who calls me that. Hey, I'm sorry if this seems nosy or something, but I saw your picture...you know, on the cover of that magazine....and, well, Glen says you get paid a lot of money. But how do you feel about *doing* that—posing like that and all? Isn't it kinda...?" His question trailed off when he couldn't find the word he was looking for. In the silence that followed James was sorry he'd come after Krin to ask her his question.

At first, Krin just looked down at her feet and pushed a leaf around with the toe of her sandal. Then she answered him. "Look, J. You're a nice kid...a really nice kid...I can tell. Let me answer your question this way. I come to these parties, stay for ten minutes, then leave. I won't stay; I *can't* stay."

Pornography

Take Another Look

How would you define pornography?

What rationale do people who support pornography offer in defense of it?

How does pornography relate to violence in our culture?

What about pornography makes James uncomfortable?

How is pornography a violation of the beauty of the human body that God created?

"Stay awake and pray that you may not come into the time of trial; the spirit indeed is willing, but the flesh is weak."

Matthew 26:41

Prayer

Derek was a freshman in high school and was going to be confirmed in three months. He had to do three major things as part of his preparation to celebrate the sacrament. He had to select a Confirmation name and write a paragraph explaining why he selected that name. He had to do a service project and discuss it with his Confirmation director. And finally, he had to interview someone about prayer and write a report on what he learned.

Derek had chosen the name "Joseph" for his Confirmation name because he thought Joseph was a great guy, supporting Jesus and Mary, and being a person of faith when things seemed weird. For his service project, Derek had learned sign language so he could help people with hearing impairments understand the homily at Mass each weekend. He still needed to do his interview, and he was going to interview his father about prayer.

DEREK: Dad, I'm not sure how to do this...I mean, it seems kinda silly to me, and all. It's, like, prayer is prayer. I don't know how I'm supposed to interview you about prayer when there isn't much to it. But...let's see. Why don't you just start by saying what prayer means, like, what is prayer?
DAD: Well, son, prayer can mean a lot of different things—at least it means a lot of different things to me. But Jesus taught us about prayer, you know, and maybe that's the main thing we should think about.
DEREK: Jesus taught us about prayer? I didn't know that. What'd he say?
DAD: Jesus' followers knew that he prayed a lot, so they asked him to teach them to pray...and he taught them the Our Father. So if you want to learn about prayer, take a good look at the Our Father sometime. Really think carefully about what we pray for when we say the words...words that Jesus himself gave us.
DEREK: Is that how you pray, Dad...you just say the Our Father?
DAD: Oh, I don't exactly pray the Our Father...except at Mass, of course...but that, I guess I'd have to say, is the most important prayer for me—the Mass. I like getting together with other people who share my beliefs and praying with them, and the Mass does that for me. Plus, there's the real presence of Jesus at the Mass.
DEREK: So you pray once a week, Dad?
DAD: No...I'm just saying that for me, the Mass is the most important prayer. But I pray a lot when I'm...well...fishing, for example. You know, there are long stretches when the fish aren't biting and everything is just still and quiet. That's when I see life all around me and I start to think about how great it all is...and pretty soon, I'm thanking God for creation..and that's prayer too.
DEREK: So prayer can happen without you being on your knees with your hands folded, huh?
DAD: Oh sure....in fact, a *lot* of prayer happens in *lots* of different ways. Take your mom. Remember when we drove out to Denver this past summer? Well, through the night hours while I drove, she sat there next to me with her rosary in her hands. She was praying there in the car, moving 65 miles per hour down the interstate.
DEREK: Wow, that's kinda cool, Dad. I didn't know that about Mom.
DAD: Oh sure. She has her rosary in her coat pocket all the time, so she can pray...anywhere...

53

Prayer

say, at the grocery store. While she's standing in the checkout line, she can slip her hand in her pocket and pray the rosary. She really loves the rosary. Then there's your Uncle Tim—now, he likes to meditate.

DEREK: You mean, like, on the floor, sitting stiff as a board, and saying "Om"?

DAD: It might be something like that...I'm not sure. I know he gets up real early every morning, when the house is dark and quiet, to put himself in the presence of God. I don't know about the "Om" part or what really goes on, but he's been a different person since he started to do that years ago. He's just much more calm and peaceful and kind. He even goes on meditation retreats.

DEREK: What about asking for things in prayer, Dad? Do you ever do that? I mean, remember when Aunt Glenda was pregnant, and we all prayed that she and the baby would be okay...and the baby died? It's like God wasn't interested in answering our prayers.

DAD: You've hit on a really difficult subject because no one really knows what God does with our prayers. We know God hears our prayers—whether we're praising God, thanking God, being sorry for our sins, or asking for something. But when it comes to specific answers to specific things that we pray about, I think God starts with loving us and goes from there. And since God is really so far beyond anything we can grasp, the love God has for us is beyond anything we can grasp too. So when we think about how God answers prayers, we just have to think about how great God's love is for us and believe that God answers with love...whatever the answer might be. You might look at it this way, son. I remember a time when you were about two years old. Your mom was fixing hot chocolate and you got so excited that you reached up on the stove to grab the boiling pot. Your mom quickly grabbed your hand away and said, "No, Derek! Don't touch. Hot! That will hurt you." I think God does something like that sometimes. Knowing us and loving us, God might decide to say "no" sometimes, and we'll never really know what God's reasons are. Our faith tells us, though, that the reasons are loving reasons.

DEREK: Do you ever just *talk* to God, Dad?

DAD: Oh sure...and if you're wondering if that's prayer, you bet it is! In fact, you might say that prayer is any kind of communication with God. We can just talk with God, out loud or in our hearts...or we can write a letter to God...or write a letter to ourselves that we might get from God. When we turn our minds and hearts to God in any way, we're praying.

DEREK: So...do you think we could say that our talking like this is prayer?

DAD: I'm sure some people would think so.

• • • • •

Derek enjoyed interviewing his dad about prayer, so much so that he wanted to find out what other people thought. He also talked about prayer with his mother and his next-door neighbor.

Derek felt good about the way his report turned out. He reported on the different ideas that people had about what prayer is, on different kinds of prayer, and on different ways to pray. He made special mention of his mother praying the rosary and his father praying while he fishes. He concluded his report by saying, "I'm not sure if this is true or not, but I want to believe that God answers all prayers in some way, always with love."

Prayer

Take Another Look

How does Derek's father define prayer?

What different kinds of prayer does Derek's father mention?

What different ways to pray does Derek's father mention?

What does prayer mean to you?

What do you think about prayers that don't seem to be answered?

*Take delight in the LORD,
and [the LORD] will give you the desires of your heart.*
Psalm 37:4

Prejudice

Brenda lived in a nice neighborhood with her two older sisters and her mom and dad. She lived close to her school, and her best friend, Ellen, lived around the corner. Brenda was a sophomore in high school and made good grades. She was president of the debate club and had just gotten a part-time job at the local library.

Brenda saw Elvir mowing the lawn in front of the house at the end of her block. She recognized him from her sophomore history class. He was a "new kid." Brenda knew that Elvir and his family were from Bosnia, where their home had been destroyed and their lives were in danger. A local civic organization had sponsored Elvir and his family and had made it possible for them to come to the United States to start a new life.

Brenda wondered what that must be like—to lose everything you value and to flee in fear for your life. She shuddered. She also felt sorry for Elvir. His English was poor, he didn't wear cool clothes, and he sure didn't have any friends. She decided she'd offer him her friendship.

Within a few weeks, Brenda grew to like Elvir a great deal. He was willing to share his life experiences and to learn everything Brenda could teach him about the American culture.

"So, are you going to Mitch's Halloween party on Saturday?" Ellen asked Brenda on the way home from school Thursday afternoon.

"Yeah, sure. Wouldn't miss it. I'll be late, though. I have to work and I don't get off until eight o'clock. So, save me a piece of pizza, will ya?" Brenda responded with a smile.

"What are you going to wear?"

"I haven't decided yet. Do you think everyone's going in costume? I'm not sure I really want to."

"Oh, come on, Bren. That's part of the fun—trying to dress so people don't recognize you and they have to guess. My dad's helping me put together a mechanic's outfit. You know, coveralls, tool belt, grease for my face, a wig, a hat. If I can get it to work, no one will ever guess it's me."

Brenda thought about Elvir. She knew he hadn't been invited to the party. Even though he'd been in school nearly two months, he still had no friends—in fact, very few people even talked to him.

"El, what do you think? What if I asked Mitch if Elvir could come to the party? Do you think Mitch would be cool with that?"

"Oh, I don't know, Bren. I guess it would be okay. I mean, it never hurts to ask about things, you know. But you'd be making it tough for Mitch. He may not want Elvir to come just because.... Well, you know. But since Mitch likes you, he'd have a hard time saying no. Do you want to put Mitch in a squeeze like that?"

"I don't want to put anyone in a squeeze," Brenda said, "but I don't like seeing Elvir miss out on fun times. He's hard to understand and he's not real cool with the way we do things yet, but if he doesn't get the chance to join in and do things, how's he ever going to fit in?"

"And you think his 'fitting in' is something you have to take care of? Come on, Bren. It's

Prejudice

not like Elvir is a little boy. And it's not like he's the only Bosnian in town. There are lots of other Bosnians here too, you know, so he just has to figure it out for himself."

"But I don't want to be prejudiced, El. I don't think Elvir should be ignored just because he's different. I want to be fair."

"Fair. Okay, be fair to Elvir. Look at it this way. He's probably never been to a Halloween party in his life. Here you want him to go to a party where he has to dress up and join in the fun of being a fake when he can't even join in the fun of being himself. You really wouldn't be doing him any favors, even if you asked Mitch and Mitch said he could come. You'd actually be making him go through something awful. It's hard enough for some of us to dress up and be something we're not. Imagine what that would be like for someone like Elvir. He wouldn't know how to act all dressed up—he wouldn't know how to act even if he weren't all dressed up. You'd just make things hard for everyone, Bren—for Elvir, for Mitch, for the rest of us. And you'd feel absolutely awful if Elvir had a really rotten time because someone said the wrong thing. And someone might, you know. Parties can get crazy, especially this kind of party where everything starts off kinda wild. I just think you're trying to do a good thing that won't turn out good at all."

"Gee, I hadn't thought of it that way, El. I was just thinking about Elvir being left out of things. I just wish he could start having some of the good times we have. But if he went to Mitch's party, that really wouldn't help at all, I guess. I'd actually be taking a big risk—he could get hurt. You're right. There's no telling what someone might say. They might not even intend to be mean, but they might still say something that could really hurt Elvir's feelings or make him mad. And it would be so hard to get him to understand. Plus, people could get mad at me for bringing him and making them feel uncomfortable—and that's not fair, is it? I guess I'd kinda do everyone a favor by not getting Elvir invited."

"Yeah, just leave things alone, Bren. Everything will work out. Don't force things that just weren't meant to be. There isn't anything any of us can really do to help Elvir fit in. He has to do the work himself. Yeah, sure. Like, we have to be friendly and all, if he wants to be, but he's the one who came to us—we didn't go to him. He has to start it—and frankly, he isn't trying very hard. He hangs out with you, but that's about all. If he wants to be friends with the rest of us, he has a long way to go. That's for sure."

· · · · ·

Brenda went to Mitch's party and had a great time. She felt uncomfortable on Monday, however, when she couldn't talk about her good time with Elvir. She began to wonder if she had done the right thing.

Brenda was pretty sure she wasn't prejudiced, yet something about Elvir and the whole party thing made her wonder. She liked Elvir and wanted him to become part of her group of friends. But she didn't want to push. After all, friends don't push their friends to do things they don't want to do. She didn't want to make her other friends uncomfortable. She didn't want to lose friends she'd had for years because of a new friendship. But at the same time, she wanted to help Elvir.

Prejudice

Take Another Look

What does it mean to be prejudiced?

How do people act out their prejudices?

How do people hide their prejudices?

How was Jesus a victim of prejudice?

What would you do if you were in a situation like Brenda's?

For in Christ Jesus you are all children of God through faith....There is no longer Jew or Greek, there is no longer slave or free, there is no longer male and female; for all of you are one in Christ Jesus.
Galatians 3: 26, 28

Relocation

Crystal had lived in the small community of Oak Woods for fifteen years. She was born there, started kindergarten there, and was now a sophomore at Oak Woods Community High School. Crystal had many good friends, two best friends, and she was just beginning to date a junior-varsity basketball player.

Crystal's mother and father owned and operated a bookstore on the southeast corner of the town square. As far back as Crystal could remember, she spent endless hours in her mom and dad's store, reading books and, when she got older, helping customers. Business had been poor for the little bookstore in recent years, however. The huge textile plant that opened in Bright Springs, fifty miles away, had hired hundreds of people from Oak Woods. These people had moved to Bright Springs to be closer to their work.

Crystal and Diane were standing in Crystal's front yard. They had just walked home from the library.

"They won't change their minds," Crystal explained to Diane, one of her two best friends. "Mom and Dad say that we have to move to Bright Springs or go broke. The store just isn't earning money anymore, so we have to move somewhere to get the business."

"Maybe they just need to advertise more," suggested Diane, "or have more sales or get more books—there must be something they can do to keep from having to move."

"They've done everything, Diane," said Crystal. "We have to do this—and I know it's going to be just awful. I'm not going to like Bright Springs. I'm not going to make friends. I'm going to hate the school. I'm going to hate our house. I'm going to hate our neighbors. In fact, I'm kinda hating my mom and dad right now."

"Oh, I got it, Crystal!" burst Diane with excitement. "You could protest...you know, chain yourself to the bed and refuse to eat or go to school until your mom and dad promise to stay here."

"No, I have a better idea," Crystal said, joining in Diane's humor. "I'll run away—I'll just disappear. I'll hide in your basement until they're gone, then I can just become your sister. Do you think your mom and dad will notice?"

Both girls laughed.

"Thanks for trying to cheer me up, Diane," said Crystal, giving her friend's arm a warm squeeze. "I'm really bummed out about this. It's just the most awful thing that's ever happened to me. I feel like I want to cry all the time—you know? I mean, it's like someone is dying or something."

"Well," said Diane, "it is kinda like someone dying. I mean, you're losing a lot of stuff that's important to you. You're going to leave friends, your house, your school, your hometown. All that stuff is pretty important."

"And the worst part is, I feel helpless," Crystal said, wiping a tear from her eye. "I understand how hard it is for Mom and Dad right now, but what's supposed to be good for them doesn't look like it's good for me. I think they understand that, but still...it doesn't change things."

"You know, Crystal," explained Diane, "Bright Springs isn't on the other side of the universe. I mean, it's fifty miles away. How hard can it be to go back and forth from here to there? We'll both be driving pretty soon, and we can just go visit each other or meet halfway or some-

Relocation

thing. We'll figure out ways to keep in touch."

"But I don't want to keep in touch," Crystal said as her single tear turned into a sob. "I want to spend time with all my friends. I want to go to school here. I want to graduate with the kids I've known all my life. I might even want to live here the rest of my life. It just isn't fair!"

"Oooh, I hate that line," cringed Diane. "Every time I say that, my father says, 'Well, that's right—it *isn't* fair, so get over it.'"

"Do you think I'll get over this, Diane?"

"Oh, sure you will," said Diane. Then, with a sheepish grin, she added, "In fact, Crystal, you know something? I'm a little bit jealous. I mean, it could be kinda exciting, you know? I mean, look, a new place to explore. A bigger town—much more shopping. You'll be able to find a great part-time job there. And you're so much fun—you won't have a hard time making friends. You're moving to a different house—our house is so boring. In a way, I wouldn't mind if I were you."

"I've thought about all that stuff, and those are good things, I guess," admitted Crystal. "Maybe if I just focus on that stuff instead of thinking all the time about not seeing you and Kate and my other friends. But it's like—well, just think what my first day of school is going to be like. I've seen new kids come to our school, and it takes them forever to make friends. Nobody wants to make friends with them. You have to prove you're not a geek before people even talk to you—and in the meantime, everyone stands around waiting to see what the new kid does. Now *I'm* going to be the new kid everyone's watching. Oh, Diane, I just can't do it!"

"Well, Crystal," said Diane. "I don't think we have a choice."

"What do you mean, 'we'?" Crystal asked, surprised at her friend's comment. "I'm the one moving, you know."

"Well, yeah, and I'm the one *not* moving! Did you ever think of it that way?" snapped Diane. "I'm stuck here while you get to move on down the road. You're my friend the same as I'm your friend, and I'm going to miss you."

"But I'm going to miss a lot more than one person, Diane. You're the one who pointed out all the stuff I'm leaving behind."

"Well, excuse me! I got feelings too, you know, Crystal," Diane said. "This isn't all about you. If you'd stop having such a good time at your own pity party, maybe you could look around you and see that some other people are pretty upset about this too."

"Oh, no, you're wrong there," insisted Crystal. "This is all about me. You just try being the new kid in school. You just try making new friends. You just try finding your way around a new town. You just try loading up all the stuff in your room and throwing it in cardboard boxes and leaving the empty room behind. It's no fun, Diane, and it is about me!"

"Well, fine then!" shouted Diane as she started to walk away. "If you're so wrapped up in everything because it's all about you, I'll just be sure to stay out of your way. I'll be sure not to miss you one bit—and maybe we'll stay in touch, and maybe we won't."

· · · · ·

After months of planning and packing, Crystal's family was ready to move. As the loaded moving van pulled out of the driveway, Crystal and her parents followed in the family car. Crystal turned around to look, once again, at the home she grew up in. It looked lonesome. She was already homesick. But, in her imagination, Crystal could see herself and Diane having that fight in the front yard several months earlier.

Crystal smiled to herself. "That was a good fight," thought Crystal. "It made me see how special friendship is."

Relocation

Take Another Look

What feelings are involved in moving away from family and friends?

What are some of the things people lose when they move?

What are some of the things people gain when they move?

How is moving different for kids than it is for adults?

How are "new kids" treated at your school?

"...And remember, I am with you always, to the end of the age."
Matthew 28:20

Running Away

Jenelle was a freshman in high school and was just beginning to find out what high school was all about. She didn't exactly like what she was learning. Everyone seemed to belong to this club and that club or to some athletic team. Jenelle was not interested in joining any clubs or teams. She was too young to get a job, and she had few friends.

Jenelle's greatest interest was music—top-ten, R and B. She knew everything about all the popular singing groups. She knew the names of each person in each group; she knew their ages; she knew as much as she could learn about their private lives. She read all the fan magazines her parents would let her buy. She just knew that if she connected with one of those groups, she could get hired as a backup singer. She'd get to travel all over the country, be with people she really liked, and earn money.

"So, how's my favorite niece doing in high school?"

"I hate it, Aunt Faith," responded Jenelle with a scowl. "It's just so boring. Everyone's into their own thing and it's all boring."

"Well, I kinda thought you wouldn't like high school much," responded Faith. "You're a lot like me...in fact, you're more like me than your mother. When we were in school, your mom was in everything. She was in clubs, joined all kinds of teams, and was secretary of the student body. Teachers were always giving her special privileges and responsibilities. She was almost a teacher's pet kind of person. But I just didn't care about any of that stuff. I'd go home after school without her—and sometimes she didn't get home until after dinner."

"Well, I've just got other things I'd rather do," sighed Jenelle as she thought about the poster of her favorite group hanging on the wall next to her dresser.

"That's right, dear. There's nothing wrong with not wanting to join in. There's nothing wrong with being different. You know what I did? I got interested in other countries. I started reading all about some of these faraway places—some I'd never even heard of. I just loved reading about what those places looked like, what the people were like, what the weather in those places was like. It was just all fascinating. I'd dream about going to some of those places someday."

"That's it, Aunt Faith. That's just exactly it!" exclaimed Jenelle. "I want to do something like that, too. In fact, I *am* going to do that."

"That's great, honey. I've still got some of those old books from years ago. I'll bring them with me the next time I come."

"No, no. You don't understand. I don't mean I want to just read about different places. I want to go—and I am going! Listen, you can keep a secret—right?"

"Well, sure," Faith assured Jenelle.

"Time and Time are coming to town next month. They're my very favorite group, Aunt Faith, and I've got a ticket to go see them. And you know what I'm going to do? I'm going backstage after the concert and apply for a position with them. I just know that if I can talk to Bick Tenner—he's their lead—that he'll see I can really be a big help to them. I mean I can help with publicity, scheduling, crowd control. I'll even do laundry and cleaning and cooking—you know, stuff like that. I've got it all planned. If I can talk to Bick, I'll be in, I know. If I can't

Running Away

talk to Bick, I'm just going to hitchhike to Kansas City. That's where they're playing next. I'll take my chances there—see if I can get a chance to talk to Bick. If I can't, then I'll just hitchhike to the next city on their tour. And I'll keep on doing that until I get my chance...and I

Won't it be wonderful? I'll get in touch with Mom and Dad once I get on with the group.

just know I will. Now you can't tell Mom and Dad...or anyone."

Faith stared at the floor for a long silent moment. "Jenelle, you're really excited about this, I can see."

"Oh, I sure am, Aunt Faith...and I just knew you'd understand!"

"Well, now wait a minute," said Faith. "I'm not so sure I understand. I'm just saying that I can see how important this is to you. You really like this group and you'd love the opportunity to travel with them, help them out, and see some of the world."

"That's right! Exactly. Won't it be wonderful?" exclaimed Jenelle. "I'll get in touch with Mom and Dad once I get on with the group...and you too, of course, Aunt Faith."

"Have you talked to anyone about your plans, dear? Anyone at all?" asked Faith.

Jenelle laughed. "Of course not! That would be crazy. That would be the stupidest thing I could do."

"Why?" asked Faith.

"Because they'd try to stop me."

"And why do you think someone would try to stop you, Jenelle?" asked Faith.

"Because...because...no one else would think it's a good idea. They'd think I was crazy. They'd try to tell me how hitchhiking is dangerous, how I'd be out of money in no time, how the group would never be interested in taking on a fourteen-year-old kid, how much my parents would worry, how I'd be breaking the law, how I'd be homesick and scared, how I wouldn't have anyone to help me if things didn't go right, how I'd miss out on getting my education...you know, all that stuff."

"I see and, well, I think you're probably right," said Faith. "Anyone trying to talk you out of this would probably say every bit of that. It sounds like maybe you've even said it to yourself, Jenelle. You've really thought the whole thing through, haven't you?"

. . . . . .

A week before the Time and Time concert, Faith called Jenelle to say that she had purchased a ticket for the concert and that she'd like to go with Jenelle. Jenelle was thrilled!

Running Away

Take Another Look

Why does running away seem like a good idea at times?

Who could you talk to if you felt like running away?

Why is running away against the law?

What would you say to Jenelle if she told you her plans?

How is running away against the Fourth Commandment: "Honor your father and mother?"

Therefore, my beloved, be steadfast, immovable, always excelling in the work of the Lord, because you know that in the Lord your labor is not in vain.
1 Corinthians 15:58

Shoplifting

The summer was drawing to a close. It was time to begin planning for school, and Todd, Jason, and Nick were school shopping together. Best friends since fifth grade, they were going to be juniors in high school.

During the summer, Todd and Nick had worked at Midway's, the local department store. Jason had worked at a video-rental store across the street from Midway's. They'd had a good time during the summer—going to parties, camping, taking their lunch hours together. All three of them had been reliable employees. Their bosses thought they were great workers and had asked them to help out later in the year over the holidays.

"Either I'm really really starved," said Todd, "or this Big Mac is especially good. Man, I mean it's good!"

"Maybe it's so good because you didn't have to pay for it, ya bum," teased Nick. "How can you do school shopping if you didn't bring any money with you?"

"Oh, no. Did I say I didn't have any money?" grinned Todd. "I meant I didn't have any money for *lunch*. I got money."

With that, Nick reached across the table and gave Todd a friendly punch. "Man, you're a loser!"

"So, where we going from here, guys?" asked Jason. "Wanna go cruise through Midway's as customers instead of being there on the job—kinda like turning the tables?"

"That's exactly what I plan to do," said Nick. "I didn't go in that place all summer except to punch the clock and hit the floor. I'm going in there to spend a little of what I earned."

"Not me," said Todd. "I'm not spending a dime in that place. It's an okay place to work, but I wouldn't spend money there. But, hey, I'll go with you. I think we can all get some great five-finger discounts. I know the guys who don't pay any attention to that kind of thing and we can really walk out with some great bargains, if ya know what I mean."

"Oh no, you don't," insisted Nick. "Don't be crazy. What do you want to do that for, Todd? Man, that's not right."

"Not right?" snapped Todd. "What's not right about it? I happen to know that there's nothing right about their pricing policies, man. I know what they pay for that stuff and how they mark it up. And believe me—we could walk out of there with a hundred dollars worth of junk, and they wouldn't even feel a dent in their pockets. Actually, it'd almost serve them right."

Jason looked at Todd, then at Nick. He was confused. "What is this, you guys? I thought you did a good job there all summer. You got asked back for the holidays and all that stuff. What's this about ripping them off? I mean, that's really bad!"

"It's got nothing to do with ripping them off," insisted Todd. "It's about justice. If they're going to sock it to the customer, the customer ought to sock back—that's all. I can't see anything wrong with that. I mean, look, they know that people would have to drive thirty-five miles to get to the nearest Walmart—and they know that most folks aren't going to do that. So, they take advantage of the locals. No one should be charged more than what an item is worth, and I'll tell you this—Midway's prices are far beyond anything their stuff is worth."

"So you're thinking you're just going to make them pay because they make the customer pay, is that it?" asked Jason. "I can't believe that you could work there all summer, Todd, get in

Shoplifting

good with the boss, and then think about stealing from him. I just can't believe it, man."

"I'm not talking about stealing," Todd said, spreading his words out slow and strong. "I'm talking about keeping the score even, that's all."

"Come on, Todd," Nick pleaded. "This isn't right. You do this and...say...you get caught.

> **We could walk out of there with a hundred dollars worth of junk, and they wouldn't even feel a dent in their pockets.**

You'll be in so much trouble...and I'm liable to be too 'cause I worked there too, ya know. Come on. Just forget it. We won't even go there."

"What's the matter with you guys?" asked Todd. "I think you're chicken. No, no. I *know* you're chicken. That's it, isn't it? You're afraid of getting caught. You don't care about anything but getting caught. Well, I'm not afraid of getting caught 'cause I know just where and how the customers are watched. This is a low-risk operation, believe me. Besides, think of it like a sport. I mean, ya win...ya lose. You have to take the risk. If you get away with the goods, ya got this great high...ya win! Ya get caught...well, there ya are...ya lose."

"Todd, listen to me," Jason said with finality. "I'm not going to Midway's. If you do, fine, but I'm not going with you. What's more, I don't want to hear anything about anything you do there if you do go. Ya got me, man? I'm not in on this and, as far as I'm concerned, this conversation never happened. So what about them Yankees? They going all the way to the pennant this year?"

"Smooth move, Marvin," said Todd with a sneer. "Chicken out and then change the subject. Whatever. You in, Nick?"

"No, Todd, I'm not in. I'm with Jason," declared Nick. "I don't care what this is all about, I'm not ripping off my employer. I got a good record there, and I don't want to screw that up."

"You mean you don't want to get caught. That's all you're saying, Nick, my boy," accused Todd. "You're just using some fancy talk to say 'I don't want to get caught.' If I could guarantee you two that you wouldn't get caught—actually guarantee it—you'd be in with me, I know you would. You'd get some neat stuff without having to spend that money we worked our tails off to earn—and you'd be for that, right? Am I right? But nooo. Chickens I got here. A couple of chickens."

· · · · ·

Nick and Jason watched as Todd went into Midway's. They did not return his wave. "He's nuts," said Nick. "Even if he doesn't get caught, something's just not right here. I just have this really bad feeling and I'm not sure what it is...but I know it isn't just about getting caught. And it sure isn't about justice."

"Yeah, I know what ya mean," said Jason. "I think it's about Todd. Something's going to be really different from now on, and you're right—it has nothing to do with justice or getting caught. Even if he doesn't get caught, Todd isn't getting away with anything."

Shoplifting

Take Another Look

Why do people shoplift?

Who suffers when people get away with shoplifting?

Besides being caught, what is Todd risking in shoplifting?

Why do Nick and Jason refuse to join Todd?

How is shoplifting against the Christian principles of justice and charity?

Thieves must give up stealing; rather let them labor and work honestly with their own hands, so as to have something to share with the needy.
Ephesians 4:28

Skipping School

Jim and Joe were twin brothers and juniors in high school. They got average grades and didn't participate in many extracurricular activities. Each had lots of his own friends, and they had lots of friends in common as well. For the most part, Jim and Joe found school boring. They didn't like most of their teachers and hated to do homework. They usually waited until the last minute to do research for term papers or to study for tests. Both Jim and Joe thought about going to college, but neither had a particular interest in studying anything specific.

Jim and Joe were hardworking. Each had a part-time job. Jim worked for a local grocery store and Joe worked at a fast-food restaurant. They liked their jobs. They liked the money they earned and their bosses often complimented them for their sense of responsibility and their hard work. Their after-school hours and weekends were usually spent at work.

"I'm not going to school tomorrow," Jim told Joe. "My boss said that I could pick up some extra hours this week if I could work a day shift, and I'm gonna go for it."

"That's just great, Jim. Thanks a lot," snapped Joe. "Do you realize the mess that puts me in? People at school are going to ask me all day long, 'Where's Jim?' Just what do you suggest I tell them?"

"Tell them anything you like," said Jim. "I don't care. I'm not going to miss this chance."

"What if Mom and Dad find out?" asked Joe. "We'll *both* be in trouble."

"How are they going to find out?" Jim asked. "They work—so they'll be gone before I leave in the morning, and I usually go right to work after school anyway. There's no way they'll find out unless you shoot off your big mouth."

"Yeah, right," said Joe sarcastically. "I might just do that and get us both grounded for a month. I don't know, Jim. Why do you have to do this? I mean, I'd like to earn a little extra dough, too, but the risk of getting caught just isn't worth it. Besides, you'll miss stuff at school."

"Miss stuff at school? Oh, rats. I hadn't thought of that," Jim said with a chuckle. "I'll miss all that great boredom. I'll miss all those geeky teachers. I'll miss all the fabulous fun I have with friends all day. Yeah, yeah. All of that is sure worth going to school for, isn't it? Give me a break, man."

"Why did your boss offer you hours during the school day anyway?" Joe wondered out loud. "He knows you'll have to skip. What's the matter with him?"

"There's nothing the matter with Mr. Stone," Jim said defensively. "He knows a good man when he sees one. He knows he can count on me to be there and to stay on top of things. He's got a freezer shipment coming in tomorrow morning, and he's short-handed to get it unloaded—and that stuff can't be off ice long, you know. So, he just asked kinda jokingly if I'd like to work tomorrow...and I jumped at the chance."

"He didn't even ask you about having to skip school?"

"No, idiot," snapped Jim. "Mr. Stone doesn't get into anybody's personal business. He treats me like an adult and respects my decisions. If he asks me to work and I want to and I can, then he doesn't go on to ask stupid questions about other things in my life. You know, I might just have a career in the grocery business. Just think—all the

Skipping School

hours and experience I'm getting. Why, when I graduate, I'll know as much about the business as people who've been in it for years and years."

"You know, Jim," Joe said, trying to get his brother to look at things from a different angle. "Going to school is kinda like a responsibility. If you're so responsible, you do what you're supposed to do—and you're not. You're sneaking off to do something else, and not paying any atten-

> **Going to school is kinda like a responsibility. If you're so responsible, you do what you're supposed to do.**

tion to the stuff you're supposed to do. I don't call that responsible."

"Will you get off it, Joe!" snapped Jim. "You'd think I was quitting school instead of just skipping one day. It's not like I do this all the time—or that I'll even do it ever again. It's just that this is an opportunity—a one-time thing. I have a chance to earn extra money and help out my boss. Hey, how about this? What if I promise to never, never, ever again skip school? Does that make you feel better? You can come up with something convincing to tell the people at school...like, well, like.... Oh, I don't know. Tell 'em I had to go to the dentist. Or I've got a twenty-four-hour flu bug. It doesn't matter. No one's going to know the truth so just say whatever."

"Maybe I should skip school too," suggested Joe. "If we're both not there, it'll look a little more normal. People will think that there was a family emergency or that the whole family is sick. Yeah, I like that idea."

"And just what are you going to do all day?" Jim asked his brother.

"I don't know—but it'll be great to feel so free! I can just do whatever I want. I can watch TV, play video games, sleep. Man! This is great. I can get pretty excited about this now. And you know, now that I think about it, you're right. We're not going to miss a thing—and it's just one day. Whatever we miss, we can catch up on. And Mom and Dad will never know. We'll have Emma call in for us and then write a note. Her handwriting is just like Mom's. Yeah, I like this a lot," Joe smiled as he stretched his arms up over his head.

. . . . .

The next day, Jim and Joe went through their usual morning routine. They were ready to leave for school when their parents left for work. "So you both have to work after school, right?" asked their mom.

"Yep," they answered at the same time. Knowing he wouldn't have to work until his usual time, Jim added, "But I think I might get off early tonight—I don't know for sure. I'll just see ya whenever."

As soon as their parents were out the door, Jim and Joe did a high-five with a whoop! "Okay!" they shouted together.

"So you're just gonna hang around here and veg, huh, bro?" Jim asked his brother.

"Yep. I'm just going to have me a one-day vacation. I deserve it—and the first thing I'm gonna do is call Emma and have her pretend to be Mom when she calls the school. Then I'm going back to bed. Why not!"

"Well, I'm gonna earn me some big bucks! Later!" Joe called as he went out the door.

Skipping School

Take Another Look

What are some of the reasons kids skip school?

Besides the risk of getting caught, what are the disadvantages to skipping school?

What can teachers do to discourage kids from skipping school?

What can parents do to discourage kids from skipping school?

How are skipping school and not going to church similar?

...and let us run with perseverance the race that is set before us.
Hebrews 12:1

Smoking and Drinking

Tesse and Pam were seniors in high school. They had been good friends since they met as freshmen. They had a lot in common—friends, sports, music. Both were also members of the high school drama club. It was Saturday afternoon and Tesse and Pam were on their way home from rehearsal. They were feeling good about preparations for the play. With opening night just a week away, they, their drama teacher, and the rest of the cast were busy trying to make sure that everyone knew their lines, props were finished and where they belonged, and programs were accurate. Neither Tesse nor Pam had leading roles in the play but, as their drama teacher had taught them, they knew their parts were critical to the overall presentation and success of the play.

"Tesse, that's your third cigarette since we left school," observed Pam. "I just wish you wouldn't do that."

"Come on, Pammy," said Tesse. "Don't start in on me again. I'm so sick and tired of this conversation. You're like a broken record. You're stuck at 'Don't smoke, don't drink. Don't smoke, don't drink. Don't smoke, don't drink.' It's like you're conducting your own private campaign or something."

"Well, I guess it is my own private campaign in a way," said Pam. "I happen to really like my friends and when I see them doing something that isn't good for them, I want to do everything I can to get them to stop."

"Well, you stop," snapped Tesse, "or I'm liable to just stop being your friend. Come on, give me a break. I really like you too, and I like relaxing and having a good time with you. One of the ways I do that is to have a cigarette...and maybe a beer. I mean, it isn't like I'm a chain-smoker or an alcoholic, you know."

"Think about it, Tesse," said Pam. "Why do you think there are laws about selling cigarettes and booze to minors?"

"Um...let me see now...let me think...don't tell me," teased Tesse. "Oh, yeah, I got it! 'Cause it's illegal! Am I right or am I right?" said Tesse with a giggle.

"Tesse," sighed Pam with exasperation, "you just don't take all this stuff seriously, do you? You're not thinking about what you're doing."

"I know perfectly well what I'm doing, Pam, and right now, I'm really, really busy trying to ignore you. You turn into such a bore with this stuff. I don't get it."

"Look," Pam tried to explain, "if you were about to fall off a cliff that you didn't realize was there, would I be 'a bore' if I yelled at you to be careful, there's a cliff right there and you might fall?"

"Oh, it's not the same thing and you know it," said Tesse.

"Come on, Tesse. It *is* the same thing," Pam defended herself. "You just can't see it—or don't want to see it. You're hurting yourself and you don't seem to care, but I do. I care enough to say 'Watch out.'"

"Well, fine," said Tesse, "you've said it, I've heard it, and thank you very much. Now, what are you doing tonight? Wanna go play some pool?"

"No, Tesse, as a matter of fact, I don't," said Pam sharply. "I know you—and you'll just smoke and tease the bartender, trying to get a beer. I'm just not interested in that."

Smoking and Drinking

"Oh man," said Tesse, "why can't we just relax and have a good time?"

"Tell me this, Tesse," said Pam. "Why do you smoke? Let's just focus there for now."

"I smoke because it relaxes me and it's cool," said Tesse.

"Well, why can't you look at relaxing like

> **It just makes me so mad—and even sad sometimes—when I see you hurting yourself.**

you look at eating?" suggested Pam. "When you're hungry, you don't eat a plate full of chocolate candy bars, do you? Because you know it wouldn't be good for you. Right? Well, it's the same with relaxing. Why not do something relaxing that isn't bad for you?

"And as far as being cool, smoking isn't cool—it's a crutch people use to try to make themselves *feel* cool. Kids who are *really* cool—like you— are cool because of something about them—like they're witty or they're fun to talk to—but they're not cool because of something they *do*—and especially not smoking! Has anyone you know who *doesn't* smoke said to you, 'Oooh, smoking is so cool. I really admire you for smoking'?"

"Pam, please," said Tesse, "I'm so tired of hearing this over and over from you. It's really beginning to get to me...I mean, I'd hate to see our friendship fall apart because I smoke and have a beer now and then."

"Well, it could come to that, Tesse," said Pam, "because it just makes me so mad—and even sad sometimes—when I see you hurting yourself. You're so good about taking care of yourself in every other way. You dress nice, your hair is cool, you wear neat makeup, you jog, you're always eating fruits and vegetables. Why can't you see that *not smoking and drinking* is a way to take good care of yourself?"

"See ya 'round, Pammy," said Tesse, with a flip of her wrist as she abruptly walked away.

· · · · ·

That evening, Tesse went with her mother to visit her aunt in the hospital. After a short visit with her aunt, Tesse told her mother to take her time, have a nice visit, and that she'd meet her down in the lobby. When Tesse's mother reached the lobby about twenty minutes later, she found her daughter staring at a poster on the wall. On the poster was the face of a once-beautiful young woman, but her face was covered with third-degree burns. The caption on the poster read, "If smoking ate away at your face the way it eats away at your lungs, would you quit?"

Smoking and Drinking

Take Another Look

Why do some kids think smoking and drinking are cool?

Why are smoking and drinking illegal for anyone under a certain age?

Why is it hard to listen to the good advice of others?

Why is the poster so powerful?

How can faith and prayer help a person who wants to quit smoking or drinking?

Do you not know that your body is a temple of the Holy Spirit within you, which you have from God, and that you are not your own? For you were bought with a price; therefore glorify God in your body.
1 Corinthians 6:19-20

Stealing Money from Parents

Abe had a tight schedule. He had to be at school by seven o'clock each morning for football practice and had to stay after school until half past five each afternoon for more of the same. As soon as he got home, he ate supper and started his homework. He knew that if he didn't keep up his grades, he'd be cut from the team.

But Abe didn't mind his schedule. In fact, he managed his schedule well. He loved football, respected the coach, and felt that he was a valuable team player. He had to work hard to keep up his grades, but he felt it was worth it. Even though he was only a sophomore, he was looking ahead to college. The only way he'd be able to go to college would be on scholarship money. A football scholarship was a possibility.

Abe, his two younger brothers, and his mother lived on a tight budget. Abe's parents divorced three years ago, and his mother had to work two jobs to make ends meet. They had all the necessities, but very little extra for special events and treats.

Abe was doing his homework when his mother came into his room to tell him he had a phone call. It was Grant.

"Hey, man, what's up?" Abe asked, always glad to hear from his best friend.

"Not much. I just wanted to know which class ring you picked."

Abe had avoided the display table in the cafeteria that entire day. He wanted to order a class ring, but it was just one of those things that didn't fall into the category of "necessity" for him or his family. He knew his mother would find some way to help him get the ring, but he didn't have the twenty-dollar deposit right now to place the order—and he was too embarrassed to admit it. He tried to convince himself that it was no big deal, but he wasn't very successful. He really did want a class ring.

"Ya know, man, I just never got time to put in my order. It's like I just didn't get to it all day."

"It's okay. You can do it tomorrow," Grant said. "The man's going to be there all day again. Take a close look at the burgundy one with the pearl center. That's the one I got."

"Sounds great," Abe responded, but he could feel a lump of pressure in his stomach.

After he hung up the phone, Abe tried to figure out what to do. His family's budget was something that worried him a great deal. He often thought about getting a part-time job, but that would add even more to his already tight schedule. He was afraid his grades would suffer.

He was also embarrassed about his family's financial situation. Most of the time, it just didn't come up and was, in fact, no big deal. But at times like this, he felt like a victim. Why did things have to be this way? Why did he have to go without some things that were really important to him just because they weren't especially important or necessary to the family? Surely there was some way to come up with twenty dollars. If he could just get the order placed, he could tell his mother that he owed sixty dollars in ninety days—she'd never have to know that he'd already put twenty dollars down. She'd feel like ninety days was enough advance notice and she'd see to it that the money was available. But twenty dollars right up front, right now—he

Stealing Money from Parents

knew that would be a problem.

Abe was still wide awake when he heard his mother turn off the television and go to bed. He was alone in the dark and quiet with his thoughts spinning. He really did want a class ring. He didn't want to be the only varsity football player that didn't have one. He knew his dad still had his class ring, and he wanted a keepsake like that, too, someday.

Maybe he could fake being sick tomorrow. Maybe the sales representative wouldn't come back. Maybe he could arrange to have another busy day. Maybe he should just check with his mother to see if she had twenty dollars. Yeah, and maybe there's a miracle about to happen.

The more Abe worried and the later it got, the more miserable he became. Over and over, he considered discussing things with his mother. But Abe just didn't want to see the pained look on his mother's face when he asked for something that she'd want him to have but couldn't afford. Then Abe hit on an idea.

"I have nine dollars left of my lunch money for the month. Maybe Mom will have eleven dollars. At least that's not twenty. I can skip lunch the rest of the month, no problem."

Pleased with his plan, Abe walked quietly to the kitchen drawer where he knew his mother kept her tips from her waitress job. There he found a lot of change, eleven ones, and four fives. Abe took a dollar in change, five ones, and one five. "Mom probably doesn't know exactly how much she's got here anyway," Abe thought. "She probably just throws it in here and takes it out as she needs it."

The next morning, the household was its usual hectic place, with three kids getting off to school and Abe's mother getting ready for work. Abe kept an eye on his mother for signs that she knew something. Abe was torn. Part of him hoped his mother had found that the money was missing—but at the same time, something else made him hope she hadn't noticed and never would.

Abe quickly ate his cereal, yelled "Bye," and headed out the door, slipping his hand into his jacket pocket to be sure his cash was secure. He started thinking about the "burgundy one with the pearl center" and the many other styles he knew he could pick from. He was so glad that he'd figured out a way to place the order for his class ring.

When Abe told his mother later that day that he'd ordered his class ring and would need sixty dollars to pay for it in ninety days, his mother was pleased. She asked him what it looked like and assured him that he would have the money when he needed it. "I'm not sure how much I have in my tip drawer right now, but I know there'll be sixty dollars in three months," she told him.

• • • • •

Three months later, the class rings arrived. Just as she promised, Abe's mother had sixty dollars for him to take to school the day of delivery. When he slipped the ring on his finger—a perfect fit—he remembered how he had worried about not being able to get one. Yet, here it was—and it was cool—the "burgundy one with the pearl center," with the numerals of his graduating year, and with his initials engraved inside. He was so proud of his ring! Plus, he'd come up with a plan that had worked. He smiled to himself thinking, "I didn't need to worry. Everything worked out just fine. I didn't get in trouble, I didn't get embarrassed, and I didn't miss out. And Mom used her tip money, so it all came from the same pot. It didn't matter."

Stealing Money from Parents

Take Another Look

Why are class rings important to people? What do they symbolize?

What symbols are important to you right now?

What would you have done if you were in a similar situation?

Do you think it would be a good idea for Abe to tell his mother what he did, now that he has the ring? Why or why not?

What other risks might Abe be willing to take now that he took this one?

For the wisdom of this world is foolishness with God. For it is written, "He catches the wise in their craftiness...."
1 Corinthians 3:19

Suicide

The sophomore class was in shock. The six o'clock news the night before had carried the story about their classmate's suicide.

Annie had been a vibrant person. She was well liked, had lots of friends, and loved sports. She played girls' basketball and went to most of the athletic events her school participated in. She and her family lived in a large house at the end of town. The house had been in the family for generations; in fact, Annie's father had grown up in that house.

Annie had two younger sisters and an older brother. Her older brother was in the army, and she talked about him all the time. She was proud of her brother who "is serving his country," as she used to say. She wanted to join the armed services when she graduated and had even contacted a recruiter.

John sat on the park bench, lost in his thoughts. He and Annie had been going steady for three months. They had just celebrated their three-month anniversary last week by going bowling. He'd given her a rose and she'd written a poem for him. His thoughts left him dizzy.

Did I cause this? Did I miss something? How could Annie have been so miserable and I didn't know about it? Weren't we close? Didn't we share some of our deepest thoughts— including our fears? She never said anything about some horrible fear she had. She never acted like she was unhappy or miserable. Well, yeah, she was pretty upset when her basketball team lost in the play-offs, but she got over that. And there was that fight she had with her mother about getting her hair dyed. But that was no big deal. Oh, and I remember how worried she was about that lost reference book. She was so afraid she was going to have to pay for it. She'd taken it from the library without anyone knowing—intending to return it the next day—and then she lost it. Funny thing about that. I couldn't seem to convince her—no one knew who took the book, so how could she be made to pay for it?

I don't know. Maybe I did cause Annie to kill herself. We had that big fight two weeks ago…over nothing. She thought I said something about military people being stupid—and I guess I did say something like that. She got really mad…and I couldn't blame her. I mean, she was really proud of her brother. I apologized right away, but it took days for her to forgive me. That wouldn't make her so miserable that she'd kill herself—would it?

Maybe I shouldn't have been all over her every time we were by ourselves. I would have never done anything serious. I just wanted to kinda make out. She'd be okay with it for a little while, then she'd want us to quit and go do something. I never liked that much, but I always went along with it. Would something like that make a person so miserable that she'd commit suicide?

Maybe I should have been more supportive when her cat got hit by a car. I just didn't think it was any big deal, but she was pretty upset. I didn't tease her about her emotions or anything, but I didn't exactly sympathize with her. I just can't imagine someone killing themselves because the cat died.

Maybe I should have called her more often. She really liked me to call her on the phone and I could have done that more often.

Maybe I shouldn't have told her about my dream to be world-cup skydiver. She really wigged out over that, like it was something hor-

Suicide

ribly dangerous and stupid. She didn't want me to have that dream and I told her that no one could take your dreams away. I told her that even if I never became a skydiver, I could always hang on to the dream.

Maybe her boss at work got on her case again. She was having a hard time learning how

How could Annie have been so miserable and I didn't know about it?

to operate the new computerized cash register, and her boss was always complaining about all the mistakes she kept making. But she seemed to be able to brush the guy off. Would that have really upset her to the point of wanting to end it all?

Maybe she was on drugs. Her friend Angie was starting to do some illegal drugs and tried to get Annie to take some, but she wouldn't—at least that's the last I heard. Maybe she got into that stuff and it just fried her brain.

Maybe she got in trouble with the law. We talked about that time when she stole a candy bar from the grocery store when she was ten years old, and got caught. Maybe she tried some of that again—and got caught, and just couldn't face it.

Maybe life was boring or scary to her. Surely she would have shared some of that with me. Surely we would have talked about something like that—or I would at least have seen some of that boredom or fear in her. I just didn't see anything like that.

Maybe there's some kind of deep, dark, and terrible secret buried in her family history and she just found out about it and just couldn't live with it.

Maybe she was really sick with something bad and she didn't tell me because she didn't trust me enough.

Maybe she wanted to break up with me and just didn't have the heart.

Maybe she flunked all her midterms last week.

Maybe she's started something. Maybe some of my other friends are going to commit suicide too.

Oh, my God!

• • • • •

Later that night, John's mother asked him how he was doing. "Oh, I'm doing okay. I'm still pretty shook up, but I'll be okay. I'm sure going to miss Annie. This whole thing is really awful."

"Do you want to talk about it a little?" John's mother asked.

"Na. Talking won't do any good. We just have to go on. I think I'll go over and see her family tomorrow for a while. Otherwise, really, I'm okay."

Suicide

Take Another Look

What are some of the emotions we feel when we learn of the suicide of someone we know?

What would you say to John if he shared his thoughts with you?

What could John's mother have done to encourage John to talk about Annie's death?

Who could you ask to help you deal with the suicide of a good friend?

What would you do if someone you knew talked about committing suicide?

*For the LORD will be your confidence
and will keep your foot from being caught.
Proverbs 3:26*

Superstitions

Gretchen and Lynn were good friends. They lived in the suburbs and caught the same train to school every day. They liked to get to the station early so they'd have time to talk before the train arrived. They talked about friends, homework, parents—in fact, there wasn't much they didn't talk about. Gretchen had five brothers and sisters, and lots of aunts, uncles, and cousins. Her family was always gathering for holidays and special occasions. Lynn had an older brother and no aunts, uncles, and cousins. When Gretchen's family got together for special events, Lynn sometimes joined them.

As sophomores, Gretchen and Lynn were beginning to look forward to high school graduation and what they wanted to do after that. They talked about moving into the city, finding good jobs, and getting an apartment together. They liked sharing their ideas about the future—and they especially enjoyed dreaming about their apartment in the city.

"You look bummed today, Gretch. What's up?" Lynn asked while they waited for the train one Monday morning.

"Oh, nothing. Well, yeah, it is something. I'm worried about my grandma. She got real sick on Saturday morning and was rushed to the hospital. No one knows what's wrong with her. She's got all kinds of pain, a fever, no appetite...I'm just really worried. My mom and dad were at the hospital all weekend with her and when they came home last night, they looked awful."

"Oh, no. That's too bad. Is there anything I can do?" Lynn asked gently.

"Well, just hope Grandma gets better—and don't do anything stupid."

Lynn wasn't sure what Gretchen meant. "Don't do anything stupid?" she asked.

"You know, Lynn. Don't let a black cat walk in front of you. Don't walk under a ladder. Don't open an umbrella in the house. Don't turn a clock backwards...that kind of thing."

"Gretch! What are you talking about?" asked Lynn. "That's all crazy stuff. That sounds like superstitious junk."

"Don't say that!" Gretchen yelled. "It's not superstitious junk—it's true! Those kinds of things are real and they do make a difference in what happens to us every day. I see it happen all the time. Look, I've got my special four-leaf-clover key chain with me today. I'm going to rub it all day so that Grandma will get better."

"I don't believe this—I just don't b-e-l-i-e-v-e this!" said Lynn "You can't be serious, Gretch. Things like that don't have any kind of power—believing they do is superstition and it's nonsense. They're just things—plain old worthless objects that stupid people think have power. You're not that stupid."

"No, I'm not stupid," insisted Gretchen, "and I know what I'm talking about. All day long on Friday, I was real careful about everything—it being the thirteenth and all. I didn't do anything stupid, but I was still worried. I was really worried at the party 'cause that's when things can happen. People don't pay attention—and sure enough, something did happen. Grandma was perfectly healthy until the party that night. We had this big cookout for my cousin's birthday,

Superstitions

and everyone was there and Grandma was fine. She even played volleyball with us—and that's when it happened. My cousin Pat took off to chase the ball and this black cat came out of nowhere and ran right in front of her. I saw it happen and I just knew it—right then, I knew it! Something terrible was going to happen. I yelled at Pat to turn around and run back, but I guess she didn't hear me. I was so worried the rest of the night—and for good reason now, obviously. Grandma is really sick. I'm just so worried and so are my parents—and the rest of the family. I've just got to make sure Grandma gets better and I'll do what I can—and if you're really my friend, you'll help me."

"Wait, Gretch. Slow down here," said Lynn, trying to be understanding. "Your grandma could be sick from anything. People get sick all the time—just out of the blue. Maybe she ate something at the cookout that was spoiled or something. Maybe she just overdid it, playing volleyball with you guys. Maybe it's a virus she picked up at the hospital where she volunteers. I mean, people get sick for all kinds of reasons—thousands of reasons, and sometimes, we never know why—but they don't get sick because a black cat shows up. Come on, Gretch."

"Why are you acting this way, Lynn?" asked Gretchen. "You're supposed to be my friend. Some friend you are...calling me names and making fun of me and not believing what I say. This is not nonsense. If you know what's good for you, you'll listen to me. And if you want to help my grandma get better, you'll listen to me. Oh yeah, and remember the B I got on my biology test last week? Well, guess how that happened. I didn't study the night before, and I got a B! I didn't get an F, and you know why? Because I had my key chain with me! I know what I'm talking about."

"Oh, no, no, no, Gretch," insisted Lynn. "You're good in biology. You always get As. It was no good-luck charm that kept you from getting an F. You got a B instead of an A because you didn't study, and you got a B instead of an F because you're good in biology. You got a B on the grading scale—that's how many questions you got right. It's that simple! It had nothing to do with your good-luck stuff."

"But I didn't study!" Gretchen nearly yelled. "I should have failed!"

"Oh, come on, Gretch. A key chain did not get you that B," said Lynn, "and a black cat did not make your grandma sick. You got a B and your grandma got sick because that's just the way things happen sometimes."

The girls stopped talking as they heard their train quickly approaching down the tracks.

• • • • •

By Wednesday afternoon of that week, Gretchen's grandmother was home from the hospital. Her illness had been caused by a serious intestinal virus. She took prescription medications for five days and was able to return to her normal routine.

Gretchen and Lynn slowly lost their close friendship, however. They met at the train station each morning as usual, but they quit sharing what was important in their lives. They didn't talk about friends, homework, or parents—in fact, they didn't talk much at all. Lynn didn't want to bring up the subject of superstitions because she was afraid she'd make Gretchen angry, and Gretchen never again invited Lynn to join one of her family's gatherings. By the time they graduated from high school, they were more strangers than friends.

Superstitions

Take Another Look

What is superstition?

What causes people to be superstitious?

What would you say to a friend who displayed a belief in superstition?

How can superstition be damaging to one's life?

What is the difference between superstition and faith?

Now faith is the assurance of things hoped for, the conviction of things not seen.
Hebrews 11:1

Talking with Parents About Tough Issues

Doug and Tina were walking together across the parking lot toward the parish center. A meeting had been called to organize the canned-food drive that the parish youth group was sponsoring for Thanksgiving.

They enjoyed belonging to St. Anthony's Youth Force. They felt the group made major contributions to their parish and their community. And, of course, they liked the social events—the lock-ins, Christmas caroling, and the spring dance.

When Doug and Tina walked into the meeting room, they saw Selma sitting on the floor next to the wall. She wasn't joining in with the other kids.

"Hey, what's up?" Doug asked as he and Tina walked over to Selma and sat down on the floor with her.

"Oooh, I'm so mad!" growled Selma. "My mother won't let me go visit my sister at college next weekend."

"That would be so much fun!" said Tina. "Why won't your mother let you go?"

Selma rested her chin on her knees and sighed. "She just doesn't trust me. She thinks I'm going to have sex, do drugs, and act crazy the whole time I'm there. She just doesn't want my sister and me to have a good time. She's always grilling my sister about what she does with her free time—telling her that she ought to get a job 'to earn money and to stay out of trouble.' She just doesn't get it."

"What does she think your sister is doing?" asked Doug.

"Who knows...who cares," snapped Selma "She just wants to keep me behind locked doors all my life. She doesn't think I can use my own judgment about some things. I mean, it isn't like I do all that stuff when I'm home, so why would I be doing that kind of thing any other time?"

"Have you tried to talk with your mother?" asked Tina.

"Oh, good one, Tina! Sure," sneered Selma. "Like, I can just see it. 'Hey, Mom, how about a little mother-daughter chat, just you and me?' Sure thing. She'd start off assuming that I was in trouble."

"Come on, Selm," encouraged Doug. "It doesn't sound like you're giving your mom a chance. She's probably just worried about you because there are some pretty crazy stories, you know, about college campuses."

"Yeah," agreed Selma, "but she doesn't have to assume the worst about my sister and me."

"Well, then, that's one good thing you could say to her," suggested Tina, "especially if you can stay calm. You know, sometimes parents just need to hear some reassuring things from their kids."

"But I wouldn't even know how to begin," said Selma, taking some hope from Tina's and Doug's encouragement.

"Well, when I want to talk to my parents about something, Selm," Doug offered, "I take the old TAN and FAN approach."

"What does that mean?" asked Selma and Tina at the same time.

"TAN—Time, Attitude, Name the problem," said Doug with a grin. "First, I make sure my timing is good...and that's no big insight, you know. Ya don't try to talk with your parents when they're trying to balance the checkbook, fix the overflowing toilet, or fighting. No rocket science in figuring that out. Then I make sure my attitude is good. I try not to go into the discussion thinking about how mad I'm going to be if I don't get my way. I try to be open and willing to hear what my parents say. And I'm ready to name the problem. It's so funny, ya know.

Talking with Parents About Tough Issues

Sometimes when I'm upset, I don't even know exactly what's making me mad. So I try to figure out exactly what I'm upset about so I can say exactly what I want to talk to them about."

"Hmm," pondered Selma. "TAN—Time, Attitude, Name the problem. I can remember that. What's FAN?"

Sometimes parents just need to hear some reassuring things from their kids.

"Facts, Assurances, Negotiations," said Doug. "Once we're talking, I offer facts. So, like in your case, you tell your parents what you and your sister are planning to do—and be specific. 'Jan and I are going to tour the campus. I'm going to her Saturday class with her, and we're going out for pizza with some of her friends on Saturday night. We'll be back at the dorm by 11 o'clock.' You can also tell your parents what you are not going to do. 'I'm not going to any wild parties, or do anything crazy.' Then offer assurances, like 'I'll call you when I get there.' Or, 'I'll call you when we get back from having pizza.' You know what would assure your mom that you're being good, or whatever. Then—and this is the biggy—be ready to negotiate. So, like, maybe your mom won't let you go for the full weekend. Maybe you can only go for Saturday—or Friday night and come home Saturday night. Maybe she'll insist on going with you...but you'd still have time with your sister to do some pretty cool things. See what I mean?"

"Wow, Doug," said Tina, "that makes sense. TAN and FAN—that's really easy to remember."

"Well," cautioned Doug, "it isn't like a magic formula. I mean, like, sometimes parents just have to 'pull rank,' as my mom says. Then it's, 'I'm the parent. Period.' But most times TAN and FAN help."

"Ya know, Selm," said Tina, "when I wanted to get my driver's license, my mom was just a wreck. She got really nervous any time we talked about me driving. And I'll always remember something she said to me one time when we were going somewhere together and I wanted to drive. She said, 'Tina, let's work on this together.' She said she had to get used to the idea of me driving and that I had to help her with that—that was part of my responsibility too. I'd just never thought of it from her point of view."

. . . . .

When Selma got home from the youth group meeting, her mother was sitting on the couch reading the paper. Selma asked her mother when they could talk about her visiting her sister at college. Her mom was willing to talk right then.

Talking with Parents About Tough Issues

Take Another Look

What are some of the emotions parents and kids have when they're trying to talk something through together?

What are the strengths in Doug's FAN and TAN approach?

What are the weaknesses in Doug's FAN and TAN approach?

Why is your own attitude extremely important when having a tough talk with your parents?

Write a short prayer to say before you talk with your parents about a difficult topic.

*Be strong, and let your heart take courage,
all you who wait for the LORD.*
Psalm 31:24

Vandalism

Gail and Jenny were juniors in high school. They'd been good friends since their freshman year when they were in the same English class. Both had earned poor grades in English that year and had to go to summer school. During those long hot weeks, they would walk to school together and then head for the public pool in the afternoon. At the beginning of their junior year, they volunteered to be co-chairpersons of the junior class homecoming float committee.

For weeks, Gail and Jenny worked to recruit volunteers to help build the float. They organized fund-raisers to finance the float and convinced Mr. Hanson, the owner of a local car dealership, to let them use an empty garage to work on the float.

It was the Thursday night before homecoming weekend. Except for a few final touches, the float was ready for Friday night's parade. Gail, Jenny, and the other volunteers were proud of their hard work. They were sure that the float would make a good showing for the junior class.

"How late did you stay last night?" Gail asked Jenny as they walked toward the garage to take a look at the float.

"We all left at 9 o'clock," Jenny answered. "We still have to figure out how to hang the banner on the side, but other than that, we got everything else finished."

Gail stopped short. "Oh, no, Jen. The padlock is broken. Was it okay when you left last night?"

"Yeah. There were just three of us working late, and we all left together. I locked up myself."

Gail removed the broken padlock and slid the garage door open. Both girls gasped. The garage looked like a tornado had ripped through it. Crepe paper, artificial flowers, boards, and chicken wire were strewn all over the garage. Their beautiful float had been totally destroyed. Spray painted on the floor of the garage and smeared with broken raw eggs were the words, "NICE FLOAT!"

"Oh, no," Jenny said through her tears. "I can't believe it. Who could have done this?"

Gail stood frozen at the entrance to the garage, shaking with rage. She couldn't believe what she saw either—but words failed her. She couldn't move. It was as if she thought that if she didn't go into the garage, what she was seeing wouldn't be real. But it was real. Their float was a pile of rubble, and it was obvious that there would be no way to repair the float before the homecoming parade the next night.

"Hey, girls," called Mr. Hanson as he walked up to the garage. "How's it going?"

Neither of the girls said anything in reply as Mr. Hanson entered the garage and saw the destroyed float. "What is this? What's happened here?"

"The padlock was smashed when we got here, Mr. Hanson," Gail explained. "Jenny, Chad, and Crystal worked late last night, but Jenny locked up before they all left." With that said, Gail broke down in deep sobs that shook her entire body.

"Come on, girls. Let's go to my office," said Mr. Hanson.

Vandalism

Gail and Jenny followed Mr. Hanson into his office where he called the police and Mrs. Sheffield, the school principal. In ten minutes, a squad car pulled into the parking lot, followed by Mrs. Sheffield's old pickup.

In response to Officer Mann's questions, Jenny gave details about the work that she, Chad, and Crystal had done on the float the night before. No, she hadn't seen or heard any-

> **Why would anyone do something like this? It doesn't make sense.**

thing unusual during that time or when she locked the garage.

No, the girls hadn't heard anyone threaten to destroy the float. No, they didn't think there was any rivalry among the grades to create the best float. No, neither one of them could think of any personal enemies who might want to get back at them. No, no one on the float committee seemed disgruntled.

Officer Mann's next questions were for Mr. Hanson. No, he hadn't seen or heard anything that made him suspect that this might happen. He didn't know of any unsatisfied customers, and none of his employees seemed unhappy with their jobs.

The group then returned to the garage while Officer Mann took a thorough look at the destroyed float and the message spray painted on the floor. He made a lot of notes, took some pictures, and said that an investigation would have to be made. He asked everyone to report to him if they thought of anything more he should know or if they heard of anything that might help out in the investigation.

After Officer Mann left, Gail and Jenny talked with Mrs. Sheffield and Mr. Hanson. Angry, hurt, and confused, the girls were also a little bit scared.

"I just don't get it," said Gail. "We worked so hard and had such a good time getting everything together. Why would anyone do something like this? It doesn't make sense."

. . . . .

The next morning, the community newspaper carried the story of the vandalism on the front page. The news item ended with a quote from Mrs. Sheffield: "This was a cowardly act of meanness. It proved nothing and it means nothing. Most of all, the person or persons who committed this crime did nothing but tear apart some tissue paper and chicken wire. The parade will go on...and the junior class will be proudly represented."

That night, the homecoming parade rolled down Main Street, led by the high school band, playing the school song. The freshman and sophomore floats followed, and then came Gail and Jenny, along with the rest of the junior class float committee, carrying the banner that they had planned to attach to the side of the float. The banner read, "The Junior Class Has Class." The final unit in the parade was the senior float.

Vandalism

Take Another Look

What would a vandal think his or her action would prove?

What emotions would cause a person to commit vandalism?

What is cowardly about committing vandalism?

Which of the Ten Commandments is violated in the act of vandalism?

How do you think a vandal should be punished?

For God did not give us a spirit of cowardice, but rather a spirit of power and of love and of self-discipline.
2 Timothy 1:7

Notes

Notes